In Praise of Sussex

selected and annotated by

David Arscott

with illustrations by

David Marl

Pomegranate Press
Westmeston, Sussex

For Jill
who loves the words, and the places, as I do

Also by David Arscott in this Pomegranate Press series:

The Sussex Story - 'the most comprehensive Sussex history package ever devised'
Living Sussex - 'an unrivalled everyman's guide to the wild places of Sussex'

Other Sussex books by the same author include:

Sussex - the County in Colour
Curiosities of East Sussex
Curiosities of West Sussex
Tales from the Parish Pump
The Upstart Gardener

with Warden Swinfen:

Hidden Sussex/People of Hidden Sussex/
Hidden Sussex Day by Day/Hidden Sussex - the Towns

Video narration:

Discovering Brighton
Discovering West Sussex

Cover photograph by David Arscott: *Flint walls and rectory at West Dean, East Sussex*

Back cover illustration by David Marl: *Lewes roofscape from Southover Grange Gardens*

Printed by Flexiprint Ltd, Lancing, Sussex
Copyright © David Arscott
Published in 1996 by Pomegranate Press, Church Cottage, Westmeston, Sussex BN6 8RH

British Library Cataloguing-in-Publication Data.
A catalogue record for this book is available from the British Library

ISBN 0 9519876 2 3

*O*ur Sussex of little lost Down churches and checker-work woods, where the Arun tumbles in its bed and one grey glimpse of sea can be caught from a high hilltop, is to an indefinable degree a landscape of the imagination. The county may have spawned few writers of stature (and Shelley, the notable exception, has nothing to say about it), but the deficiency has been more than made good by the countless literary 'furriners' who have trapped its rich colours in poetry and prose. This book, completing a trilogy which celebrates Sussex in the round (its history, its wildlife, its personality), is their testament.

Choices have to be made, of course, and only a cowardly anthologist would seek to shift the responsibility to his authors. Although I make no apology for concentrating on beauty rather than ugliness, my aim has been to present a recognisable rather than a traditional or romantically idealised Sussex - which is why I find little space for ancient customs or for writing earlier than the twentieth century. A thorny problem of identity remains, however. If the landscape is much as it was a hundred years ago, albeit more scarred and densely populated, we shall have to search very hard to find the distinctive Sussex character which authors commonly claimed to discern as recently as the interwar years. Our once narrow world has been invaded both by hordes of incomers (yes, I am one myself) and by a mass culture which ruthlessly scours and abrades individuality.

My solution has been to compromise. The old countryman's 'wunt be druv' stubbornness and bone-dry sense of humour may be endangered species but, as with our Sussex accent and dialect, we can yet observe their lingering traces. It would have been an act of puritanical self-denial to have withheld their gamey flavours from the stew. Similarly, I have included accounts of labouring life and of the great shepherding days on the hills, since these, too, live within the memory of our oldest inhabitants: they remind us where we have come from, and alert us (though no doubt unavailingly) to the giddy pace of change.

As for the places, a personal selection is necessarily idiosyncratic, and, since we are all intemperate about the things we love, every Sussex partisan should enjoy finding fault with it. A glance at the gazetteer will reveal its wide thematic and geographical range, but I readily concede that my favourite landmark, townscape, pub, church or garden may not be yours. Newcomers to the county, on the other hand, should find in these pages manifold temptations to explore our still green and pleasant land (to quote a poet who lived here for a spell) until they find themselves similarly qualified to take issue with the contents. For there is, still, something about Sussex - something that does, after all, amount to an identity - which draws the stranger back and speaks to the native of home.

David Arscott

ACKNOWLEDGEMENTS

Any author of an anthology is obviously indebted to the writers whose works he has raided, and I am pleased to record my gratitude here. The appreciation should perhaps be accompanied by an apology. I am aware that, in ruthlessly mining their works to suit my own purposes, I have sometimes done them far less than justice. Where a line or a paragraph appears I might have borrowed a page or a chapter had space allowed. I have drawn from as many sources as feasible in order to suggest a portfolio fit for the shelves of any ardent book-reading lover of Sussex, while admitting that a list of those I have omitted would probably prove just as long: some writers are more quotable than others. As for the editing, where I have (necessarily) left out parts of the original I have done so silently, not wishing to have the text disfigured by frequent rows of dots.

— Virginia Woolf

My thanks to all the following for their kind permission to reproduce material in this book:

Bob Copper (*Early to Rise, A Song for Every Season, Jim Copper's Songbook*); Doreen Darby (Ben Darby's *View of Sussex, Journey Through the Weald, The South Downs*); The Hilaire Belloc Estate and Peters Fraser & Dunlop (*The Four Men, The South Country, On an Unknown Country*); The Sheila Kaye-Smith Estate and Peters Fraser & Dunlop (*Sussex Gorse*); Susan Rowland (Frank Dean's *Strike While the Iron's Hot*), Len Tuppen's *Only Yesterday,* Harold Cannings's *Follow the Plough*); Tony Schilling (*The Gardener's Garden*); Tim Carder (*The Encyclopaedia of Brighton*); The Society of Friends of Ashdown Forest (Garth Christian's *Ashdown Forest*); Tony Wales (*A Sussex Garland, Sussex - Customs, Curiosities & Country Lore*); Dirk Bogarde and Random House UK Ltd (*A Postillion Struck by Lightning*); Angelica Garnett and Random House UK Ltd (*Deceived With Kindness*); Adam Nicolson and Weidenfeld & Nicolson (*Prospects of England*); J.M. Dent (Maude Robinson's *A South Down Farm in the Sixties*); Methuen (Barclay Wills's *Downland Treasure*); Reed Books (A.A. Milne's *The House at Pooh Corner*); Moorland Publishing (Jim Cleland's *Visitor's Guide: Sussex*); BBC Worldwide Limited (Alec Clifton Taylor's *Six More English Towns*); Chambers Harrap (W. Victor Cook's *The Keys of England*); Robert Hale and Michael H.C. Baker (*Sussex Scenes*); Brigid Chapman and Countryside Books (*Sussex - A Portrait in Colour*); Brigid Chapman and S. B. Publications (*Night of the Fires*); Peter Linklater and The Friends of Lewes (*Lewes Twittens*); Countryside Books (Lillian Candlin's *Memories of Old Sussex*); Little Brown (Marcus Crouch's *The Heritage of Sussex*); S.B. Publications and Jim Etherington (*Lewes Bonfire Night*); George Aitchison and A & C. Black (*Sussex*); Desmond Seward, Pimlico and Sheil Land Associates Ltd (*Sussex*).

Although I have done my best to track down all holders of copyright, I can well believe that one or two have slipped through the net. If so, I offer my regrets and a willingness to put matters right in any subsequent reprint.

My thanks, finally, to Peter Chapman, for technical help far beyond the call of a printer's duty, and to David Marl, whose evocative illustrations have beautified each part of this Sussex trilogy.

CONTENTS

We begin with the obvious, because it is undeniably the best. Does any other county have an unofficial anthem so lovingly detailed as well as so finely expressed?

We may perhaps quibble about Piddinghoe's weather vane (surely a sea trout from the neighbouring Ouse) and the supposed reliability of dew ponds during a drought, but Rudyard Kipling devoured the lore of his adopted county and travelled its dusty lanes indefatigably in a succession of much loved, but not always reliable, motor cars: one of his sturdy Rolls-Royces is on show at Bateman's.

Kipling, already famous, moved to Rottingdean in 1897, the family first sharing North End House with his uncle, the painter Edward Burne-Jones, and then moving to The Elms, by the village green. It was in 1902 that he bought the former ironmaster's house at Burwash where he was to spend the last 34 years of his life: the wonderfully atmospheric study where he wrote such works as Rewards & Fairies and Puck of Pook's Hill is littered with his writer's paraphernalia.

A few notes on the poem: Wilfrid is the saint credited with bringing Christianity to Sussex; Winchelsea and Rye are the ports stranded by a withdrawing sea; The Long Man is the striking 230ft hill figure of uncertain age; and the eastern Rother 'doubles' not only because of its sinuous course but because it has a namesake in the west of the county.

The sheep-bells were less clangorous and the red oxen (those 'Sussex steers') had stopped ploughing by the time that Kipling died.

SUSSEX

God gave all men all earth to love,
  But, since our hearts are small,
Ordained for each one spot should prove
  Belovèd over all;
That, as He watched Creation's birth,
  So we, in godlike mood,
May of our love create our earth
  And see that it is good.

So one shall Baltic pines content,
  As one some Surrey glade,
Or one the palm-grove's droned lament
  Before Levuka's Trade.
Each to his choice, and I rejoice
  The lot has fallen to me
In a fair ground - in a fair ground -
  Yea, Sussex by the sea!

No tender-hearted garden crowns,
  No bosomed woods adorn
Our blunt, bow-headed, whale-backed Downs,
  But gnarled and writhen thorn -
Bare slopes where chasing shadows skim,
  And through the gaps revealed,
Belt upon belt, the wooded, dim,
  Blue goodness of the Weald.

Clean of officious fence or hedge,
  Half-wild and wholly tame,
The wise turf cloaks the white cliff-edge
  As when the Romans came.
What sign of those that fought and died
  At shift of sword and sword?
The barrow and the camp abide,
  The sunlight and the sward.

Here leaps ashore the full Sou'west
  All heavy-winged with brine,
Here lies above the folded crest
  The channel's leaden line;
And here the sea-fogs lap and cling,
  And here, each warning each,
The sheep-bells and the ship-bells ring
  Along the hidden beach.

We have no waters to delight
  Our broad and brookless vales -
Only the dewpond on the height
  Unfed, that never fails -
Whereby no tattered herbage tells
  Which way the season flies -
Only our close-bit thyme that smells
  Like dawn in Paradise.

Here through the strong and shadeless days
  The tinkling silence thrills;
Or little, lost, Down churches praise
  The Lord who made the hills:
But here the Old Gods guard their round,
  And in her secret heart,
The heathen kingdom Wilfrid found
  Dreams, as she dwells, apart.

Though all the rest were all my share,
  With equal soul I'd see
Her nine-and-thirty sister fair,
  Yet none more fair than she.
Choose ye your need from Thames to Tweed,
  And I will choose instead
Such lands as lie 'twixt Rake and Rye,
  Black Down and Beachy Head.

I will go out against the sun
  Where the rolled scarp retires,
And the Long Man of Wilmington
  Looks naked toward the shires;
And east till doubling Rother crawls
  To find the fickle tide,
By dry and sea-forgotten walls,
  Our ports of stranded pride.

I will go north about the shaws
  And the deep ghylls that breed
Huge oaks and old, the which we hold
  No more than Sussex weed;
Or south where windy Piddinghoe's
  Begilded dolphin veers,
And red beside wide-bankèd Ouse
  Lie down our Sussex steers.

So to the land our hearts we give
  Till the sure magic strike,
And Memory, Use, and Love make live
  Us and our field alike -
That deeper than our speech and thought,
  Beyond our reason's sway,
Clay of the pit whence we were wrought
  Yearns to its fellow-clay.

God gives all men all earth to love,
  But, since man's heart is small,
Ordains for each one spot shall prove
  Belovèd over all.
Each to his choice, and I rejoice
  The lot has fallen to me
In a fair ground - in a fair ground -
  Yea, Sussex by the sea!

Rudyard Kipling: 'Sussex'

• The Long Man of
Wilmington
199: TQ 543035

• Piddinghoe Church
198: TQ 435031

Where Kipling lived:
• Bateman's, Burwash
(National Trust)
(01435) 882302
199: TQ 671238

AN OLD SUN-TANNED MARINER

Hill towns are rare in England. In Sussex Lewes is one, Winchelsea another, but Rye, its sandstone rock rising out of the total flat of the fen, makes its statement yet more unmistakably. The houses building up to the low tower of the church are reminiscent of the north of France.

Nikolaus Pevsner: 'The Buildings of England - Sussex'

I have been to the South, the far end of Florida etc - but I prefer the far end of Sussex! In the heart of the orange groves I yearned for the shade of the old Lamb House mulberry tree.

Henry James, in a letter

There is not in all England a town so blatantly picturesque as Tilling, nor one, for the lover of level marsh land, of tall reedy dykes, of enormous sunsets and rims of blue sea on the horizon, with so fortunate an environment. The hill on which it is built rises steeply from the level land, and, crowned by the great grave church so conveniently close to Miss Mapp's residence, positively consists of quaint corners, rough-cast and timber cottages, and mellow Georgian fronts.

E.F. Benson: 'Miss Mapp'

It is like no other town in England. We pass through its great gate and feel that we are in the world which set the gateway up so many centuries ago. Rye seems out of place and out of time.

Arthur Mee: 'The King's England - Sussex'

Rother would sometimes seem more than a town of old, decaying black-and-white houses huddling inside an ancient town wall - Rother would almost seem like a person. Rother could draw unto itself lovely colours: soft greys and soft browns and soft, dark purples; and at sunrise and sunset its red roofs would blaze, and so would the leaded panes of its windows; and after a storm all its cobbles would shine, while the grass in between them would look as bright as though it had just had a coat of fresh paint.

Radclyffe Hall: 'The Sixth Beatitude'

Stranded now, Rye lies by the sea her sailors ruled, and, like some old, sun-tanned mariner who has left his roving, whispers in the ear of day-dreamers of storms past and perils overcome, of voyages adventured and battles fought ages before Drake was born or Columbus sailed.

W. Victor Cook: 'The Keys of England'

'For our time is a very shadow that passeth away,' reads a quotation from the Apocrypha on the church clock at Rye. It might be a valediction to the town's glorious trading and shipbuilding days, when great merchant vessels from the ports of northern Europe tied up alongside a large fishing fleet at quaysides now two miles inland. The Ypres Tower of 1250 and the Landgate of around 1340 (not to speak of the much-filmed Mermaid Inn behind its cobbles) survive to remind us of that prosperous period: changing trade patterns and the silting of the harbour from the end of the sixteenth century doomed the port to a less illustrious future as a comfortable market town.

As so often, it is the outsiders who have written best about Rye - which, in return, seems admirably tolerant of outsiders of every kind. Radclyffe Hall was embroiled in a lurid court case over her lesbian novel The Well of Loneliness when she arrived in the town with her lover in 1928: her novel The Sixth Beatitude is set in Hucksteps Row, 'Rother'. For E.F. Benson, in his Mapp & Lucia books, the town is 'Tilling' after another local river, the Tillingham. Benson, who was to find his feline swipes at life in Rye rewarded with the office of mayor, rented Lamb House from 1919 until his death in 1940. The Garden Room, in which Henry James had written his late, great novels (with, alas, no Rye colour) was demolished by a German bomb in the last war. The mulberry tree was destroyed by a gale shortly before James's death in 1916.

— Rye —

Where Henry James and (later) E.F. Benson lived:

- *Lamb House, Rye (National Trust) (01797) 223763 189: TQ 920202*

Where Radclyffe Hall lived:

- *The Black Boy, 4 High Street, Rye (private, with plaque) 189: TQ 922204*

- *The Forecastle, Hucksteps Row, Rye (private) 189: TQ 922203*

- *The Mermaid Inn Mermaid Street, Rye 189: TQ 921204*

Rye Tourist Information (01797) 226696

Nearby attractions:

- *Camber Castle (English Heritage) 189: TQ 922185*

- *Winchelsea Church 189: TQ 904173*

See 'The Cruel Sea' in <u>The Sussex Story</u> *for the changing coastline*

See 'Of Time and Tides', 'Glorious Mud' and 'Fashioned by Wave & Wind' in <u>Living Sussex</u> *for local wildlife and nature reserves*

A PROFOUND ENGLISHNESS

Those who know the strange and powerful novels of John Cowper Powys, with their extravagant mixture of philosophy, human passion and the supernatural, may find it hard to imagine him lecturing at a girls' school in Brighton. His employers would certainly have been somewhat alarmed to learn that their young English teacher was buying erotica from a second-hand bookshop in Eastbourne, working himself into a frenzy by furtive gazing at girls' ankles on Brighton beach and giving himself up, as he would later record in his Autobiography, 'to neurotic aberrations which must constantly have wavered and toppled on the verge of madness'.

He came to Sussex in 1893, newly graduated from Cambridge, and this passage vividly describes the journey. Powys married while living at Offham, and his son was born at Burpham, where he lived but fitfully thanks to lecturing work in America and the inevitable deterioration of his marriage. His novel After My Fashion is set in Sussex.

Amberley, illustrated here, has more than its fair share of the mellow cottages that Powys writes about, and rather more thatch than is common in Sussex, too: indeed, 'an anthology of building materials - thatch and tile, brick, flint, half-timber, and Burgate stone, and also just a little clunch', to quote Ian Nairn. Add a fourteenth century castle (built for the Bishop of Chichester) and a setting between the Downs and the tranquil waters of the Amberley Wildbrooks, and you have one of our loveliest villages: 'sheer Sussex', according to E.V. Lucas.

Sussex scenery, as I now looked out on it from my third-class smoking-carriage, was certainly different from any scenery I had ever seen. Those huge Sussex barns whose vast sloping roofs were encrusted with orange-coloured lichen that was as strange to me as were the 'orange-tipped' butterflies I saw on the railroad banks, in place of our Dorset 'marble' whites, those mellow Sussex cottages where old dark woodwork was so cunningly mixed in with brickwork and flintwork, those Sussex bricks themselves that were so much brighter and gayer than the red bricks of my native Midlands and gave a look to the whole scene so much warmer and sunnier than the Dorset thatch or the Somerset stone, those enormous Sussex wagons, painted blue and scarlet, and of a size so large that they would have astonished a Somerset farmer, the trim, neat, picturesque Sussex villages themselves, where it seemed as though everyone was so much more well-to-do than in the West Country, all these things struck me, sank into me, and abode with me, as to some literary person, who has been reading Sir Thomas Browne and Thomas Hardy, it would be if he suddenly discovered a volume of Walter Pater.

It was not my country, this warm, mellow, gracious tender-soiled Sussex, just as they were not my people, these blue-eyed South-Saxons, but there was something about the place that was profoundly English; more English, in the narrowest sense of that word, than any other county in the kingdom. Yes, I liked the look of the scenery more and more as the train made its way through the hollows of the Sussex Downs, downs so much higher, wider, steeper, and in every way more formidable than the downs of my father's Dorset.

'Lewes! All change for Eastbourne!'

This particular cry, on this particular platform, how well I was to know it in later years! It was accompanied by the shrill voices of the newspaper boys selling Brighton papers, voices that had a distinct Cockney flavour, for the Sussex dialect has some ancient affiliation, which I am not enough of a philologist to analyse, with the manner of speech of England's metropolis.

Perhaps it is the accessibility of Sussex to London, together with something at once warmly gay and comfortably home-like - the 'aura', in fact, of rose-coloured bricks flecked with golden lichen - that gives to this picturesque and reassuring county its peculiar quality. The great Downs themselves, like huge waves solidified into chalk and turf, are never as desolate as their wide sheep-cropped undulations would lead you to expect. Something about their wind-swept clumps of beeches, something about their gorse-patches and beds of thyme and harebells and milkwort, softens their austerity; and from every point along their highest ridges you can see the glittering waters of the English Channel to the south, and to the north the vaporous blue haze of the great wooded Weald. Steep to ascend though these Sussex Downs are, the chalk tracks that lead down from their summits plunge a wayfarer with surprising celerity into the snug and homely villages that nestle in the hollows beneath them; while even the straggling little seaside places on their Channel side between Brighton and Worthing - Portslade, Southwick, Shoreham, Lancing - have, for all their rather ramshackle dinginess, a certain friendly and human look, suggestive of the presence of quaint Dickensian characters dwelling in those rows of little stucco houses.

John Cowper Powys: 'Autobiography'

• *Amberley Castle*
(Hotel: 01798 831992)
197: TQ 027132

Where John Cowper Powys lived in Sussex:

• *Court House, Offham*
(now Courthouse Farm; private)
198: TQ 383128

• *Bankside, Burpham*
(now Frith House; private)
197: TQ 039089

— Amberley —

DEAR CHECKER-WORK OF WOODS

If a champion were needed to fight the cause of the Weald against the Downs (mercifully an unnecessary contest) Wilfrid Scawen Blunt would be our man. This colourful and much-travelled poet, amateur diplomat, horse-breeder and Arabist was born at Crabbet Park in 1840 and was so proud of his roots that he once objected to sharing a collection of Sussex verse with those 'furriners' Belloc (a friend, as it happens) and Kipling: the lines from Chanclebury Ring are inscribed on his tomb. A fierce anti-imperialist, who was briefly jailed for supporting an independent Ireland and who would ride round his estate dressed in Arab robes, Blunt married a granddaughter of the poet Byron, on whose affairs, the Oxford Companion to English Literature wryly observes, 'his own career as amorist appears to have been modelled'.

There is, as our extracts show, no shortage of good writing about the Weald. A 'lag' (Blunt's poem) is a marshy meadow; 'Anderida' (Halsham) is properly the Roman name for Pevensey, but here signifies the great Andredsweald forest the Saxon settlers first began to tame; 'abeles' (Edward Thomas) are white poplars.

What is the Weald? Where is the Weald? Many people who actually live there could not answer these questions. Geological and geographical textbooks explain that it is the name of the great valley lying between the North Downs and the South Downs. Strictly speaking, this is true, but it is a vast over-simplification. It suggests a large green bowl sloping down from surrounding hills. Nothing could be further from the truth. The landscape is extraordinarily varied within the confines of the two downland ranges. There are tall hills and deep valleys, high ridges and flat lands and a lot of rivers. Many of the hills are much higher than the enclosing Downs.

Ben Darby: 'Journey Through the Weald'

Dear checker-work of woods, the Sussex Weald.
If a name thrills me yet of things on earth,
That name is thine! How often I have fled
To thy deep hedgerows and embraced each field,
Each lag, each pasture - fields which gave me birth
And saw my youth, and which must hold me dead.

Wilfrid Scawen Blunt: 'Chanclebury Ring'

When we came on to the shoulder of Chanctonbury and looked down upon the Weald, which stretched out like the Plains of Heaven, he said to me: 'I never come here but it seems like a different place down below, and as though it were not the place where I have gone afoot with sheep under the hills. It seems different when you are looking down at it.' He added that he had never known why. Then I knew that he, like myself, was perpetually in perception of the Unknown Country, and I was very pleased.

Hilaire Belloc: 'On an Unknown Country'

This is rather a mysterious time of the year in this part of the country. If I were to take you one evening up one of those muddy broken tracks that lead to the top of the Downs and we went plunging on through the tangled bracken and slippery grass, we would eventually find ourselves on a frosty ridge overlooking a

twilit world that sprawls eight hundred feet below; a dark country between the North and South Downs that with the coming of Christmas draws down over itself the murky cloak of Legend. This is the Sussex Weald, an ancient country of secret places, hidden villages, river sources, silent pools, dim glades and forgotten roads, all of them localities where in these darkening days Legend rears itself, taking advantage of the shadows of a winter's dusk.

Gerard Young: 'Come Into the Country'

In all English silvan landscape - taking landscape to mean not the foreground-picturesque of forest glades or undergrowth, but great wooded distances - there can hardly be anything richer than the view from the Forest Ridge southwards over the Sussex Weald. Its charm constantly has the addition of surprise: a gap in the roadside furze, or a gate between high hedges, gives a sudden outlook over the plain, rolling with swell and hollow to the grey rampart of the Downs which rise from it like island cliffs from the sea. At first sight it is all woodland: Anderida itself could hardly have stood thicker, one thinks; but after a little looking the clearings, old and new, begin to show themselves - the squares of ploughland and pasture, the roofs of farms, the rusty scar of a quarry-hole, a windmill on a heathy common, that catches a travelling gleam of sun ten miles away, a haze of smoke drifting from a little town. The view unfolds itself, plane beyond plane, every minute that it is watched.

John Halsham: 'Old Standards - South Country Sketches'

Green lucent calipers of flags shadow one another in little wayside ponds, white-railed; for this is the Weald, the land of small clay ponds. The hazels are the nightingale's. In many of the oak woods the timber carriages have carved a way through the primroses and bluebells deep into the brown clay. The larger views are of cloudy oak woods, ridge behind ridge, and green corn or grass and grey ploughland between; and of the sun pouring a molten cataract out of dark machicolated clouds on to one green field that glows a moment and is insignificant again: the lesser are of little brambly precipitous sandpits by the road, of a white mill at a crossing, of carved yews before black-timbered inns, of a starling that has learned the curlew's call perched on a cottage roof, of abeles all rough silver with opening leaf shivering along the grass-bordered evening road, of two or three big oaks in a meadow corner and in their shadow unblemished parsley and grasses bowed as if rushing in the wind.

Edward Thomas: 'The South Country'

See The Sussex Story *for the centuries of iron-making in the Weald*

see Living Sussex *for a selection of Wealden nature reserves*

Where Wilfrid Scawen Blunt lived:

• *Crabbet Park, Worth (private) 187: TQ 305373*

• *Newbuildings Place, Southwater (private, with tomb in the woods behind) 198: TQ 141245*

11

THE ROTTINGDEAN MUCKMEN

If there was one single incident in the village's more recent history which marked the most significant change it had ever  seen and which, practically overnight, transformed its entire character, it was when the farm was sold for the second time in 1928. I speak, of course, as one of the 'up-streeters' or agricultural community upon whom its effect was more dramatic than on the 'down-streeters' or tradespeople. But as Rottingdean had been predominantly agrarian for by far the greatest part of its existence, this sale was a most important milestone in its history and heralded startling changes in the living patterns of the majority of the old villagers.

Men who had spent all their lives on the farm and whose families for generations had got a living from the land, had to shake the soil from their boots and look elsewhere for a livelihood. Shepherds, cowmen and carters found that the knowledge they had accumulated in a lifetime of experience was suddenly of no further use to them and that they had to turn their minds and their hands to the timber, bricks and mortar of the building trade. For this was the new door which slowly opened after the old familiar barn doors had been shut, and as the sickles, scythes, sheep-crooks and shears were laid aside, first one and then another took up the hammer, trowel and paintbrush to provide homes for the new arrivals who were beginning to appear.

I had to help Dad as often as my attendance at school and, later, work at the barber's would allow, but there was one job which required two pairs of hands and therefore had to be arranged during the times when I was available. He had mounted a heavy, iron hand-pump on a stout, wooden, trestle-type frame with two handles at each end by which it could be carried in the manner of a stretcher. To the pump were attached two lengths of four-inch, armoured, rubber hose, which some years before had been used for filling the water-tank of the steam traction engine on the farm, and with this contraption we used to empty cess-pits at five shillings a time.

As our methods were a little unorthodox - merely running the outlet pipe over the garden fence or through the hedge and pumping the effluent out on to the nearest piece of spare ground - we usually operated after dark. So as dusk fell on the village two rather furtive figures might sometimes have been seen trudging one behind the other up the steep hillside track carrying something rather heavy between them and pausing at intervals 'for a blow'. Although it was not exactly the sort of job that could be taken lightly or conducted in a spirit of fun, I recall that there was never the slightest sense of despondency and certainly none of shame. We were doing an honest job for an honest reward and, though perhaps not the kind of task you would have done from choice, there was no need to be gloomy about it. We laughed and joked and even sang a snatch of song which was particularly appropriate:

> *My father's the old village muckman,*
> *He empties the dunnicks at night,*
> *And when he comes home in the morning*
> *He's covered all over with -----*
> *Sweet violets, much sweeter than all the roses,*
> *Take them, my darling, I plucked them on purpose for you.*

I remember once returning home over the hill carrying our foul-smelling burden between us with Dad in the leading shafts. It was a warm night with a clear, star-studded sky and the moon glittered in a silver path like a ribbon of stars fallen into the sea. 'Old 'ard a minute,' he said, 'I could do with a smoke.' We set the cumbersome equipment down on the soft, downland turf and sat on it, one on either side of the pump, both glad of the opportunity to rest.

Presently the smoke from a cigarette he had rolled with reeking fingers began to drift round us on the still night air smelling fragrant and wholesome. It was quiet and peaceful after the clanking and groaning of the pump for the last hour or so, and the thought that we were able to work together so amicably on such an unpleasant job made us realise that we had a really tremendous bond of affection between us.

'Look at that, boy,' he said, 'the King of England wun't never see a better sight than that - not if 'e travels the wide world over.' Then he started to sing:

> *Although I'm not rich and although I'm not poor,*
> *I'm as happy as those that's got thousands or more.*

We sang the song right through to the glory of the moment with no one to scoff or sneer at its quaintness, which in those days was considered by most to be dull and old-fashioned. For us the joy of the song was in the singing of it and of being together and being able and willing to do so.

'Bugger, boy' he said, when the song was ended, 'I wish you'da bin m' brother instead o' m' son - I'd 'a' known y' longer.'

Bob Copper: 'Early to Rise'

Copper family memorabilia:
• Grange Museum,
Rottingdean
198: TQ 369026

KEW IN THE COUNTRY

The acid soils of the High Weald favour outrageous spring displays from those plant hunters' delights, the rhododendrons, azaleas, camellias and magnolias, and the area abounds in gardens which have an international reputation for their collections of shrubs and trees. Each has its special features (a rugged skeleton of rock outcrop and ravine at Wakehurst Place; the blaze of autumn colour reflected in the lakes at Sheffield Park; the long view across the Weald from the terrace at Nymans; the hammerponds in the valley bottom at Leonardslee), and each has had to recover in its own way from the 'hurricane' which struck Sussex in October, 1987.

I scattered my father's ashes at Wakehurst, an indication of our shared feeling for the place, and the countless plaques on the benches strategically placed about these five hundred up-and-down acres reveal that the affection is widespread. For the Royal Botanic Gardens, who lease 'Kew in the Country' from the National Trust, the appeal is understandably more scientific. Both soil and climate are markedly different from those at sea-level Kew - as, indeed, they are from parts of Sussex only a few miles away. 'When I go home,' wrote Tony Schilling, a former curator who collected a great many of Wakehurst's exotic shrubs on expeditions to the Himalayas and who is a near-neighbour of mine on the chalk at Westmeston, 'I travel from a pH of 4.7 to one of 8.5, driving from a slow-draining silt-loam to a fast-draining alluvial outwash soil.'

The great delight of Wakehurst is its naturalness, which, in fact, owes much to human skill. Nature is guided but never bulldozed. Exotic trees, shrubs and other plants grow happily among the Wealden beeches, oaks, birches and pines. Lakes and dramatic outcrops of sandstone set off the trees and flowers.

Ben Darby: 'Journey Through the Weald'

Given the necessary resources, a good garden is not too difficult to create, but a really great garden demands a total commitment. The rewards are many, not least of these being the enjoyment Wakehurst gives to the 250,000 or more visitors who pass through its gates annually. They come seeking many things including gardening inspiration, peace of mind and intellectual stimulation, but most of all I believe they come in quest of beauty

Tony Schilling: 'The Gardener's Garden'

I have to admit with shame that until recently I had not visited Wakehurst Place since the aftermath of the great storm, to see how the Royal Botanic Gardens have recovered

Wakehurst Place — circa 1975

from the devastation, and the loss of something like 15,000 trees. The answer, of course, is ingeniously, laboriously and astonishingly.

The Wakehurst of today is a more complete botanic garden than ever it was, more artfully and horticulturally designed, more botanically organised, more full of 'visitor interest'. The site is so exceptional, plunging from the intensely sophisticated horticulture around the mansion by stages of plantations and glades, water and rocks to the lake at the bottom - and across the lake to the untamed wildwood - that one is soon carried away by the excitement of potential steadily being realised.

One corner I had never visited before is the willowbeds in wetland flooded by the lake, a self-contained landscape hemmed in by steep slopes and woods and crossed by a wholly Oriental-looking wooden causeway. This, and the dream-like view along a sinuous valley with the Ardingly reservoir gleaming at the bottom, from the high ground where a whole wood was blown down, are landscapes to memorise for inspiration.

Hugh Johnson: 'The Garden' magazine

• Wakehurst Place, Ardingly (National Trust) (01444) 892701 187: TQ 339314

Other notable gardens of the High Weald in Sussex:

• Nymans Garden, Handcross (National Trust) (01444) 400321/400002 187/198: TQ 265294

• High Beeches Gardens, Handcross (01444) 400589 187: TQ 278307

• Sheffield Park Garden (National Trust) (01825) 790231 198: TQ 415240

• Leonardslee Gardens, Lower Beeding (01403) 891212 187/198 TQ 222259

• Borde Hill Garden, Haywards Heath (01444) 450326 187/198: TQ 323266

See 'A Gardener's Life', p. 74, for a selection of gardens in other parts of the county

An eighteenth century trading boom brought Chichester a handsome Georgian face-lift, but the city's roots run far deeper. It was the Romans who designed the basic plan (a central crossing of major streets within encircling walls) which so impressed the sculptor and typographer Eric Gill when he first came here in 1897. The native king Cogidubnus, probably educated in Rome, had welcomed the invaders and was rewarded with the building of a sumptuous palace at Fishbourne. At first simply a military base from which the legions could attack hostile tribes to the west, Chichester grew into a substantial town with all the amenities a citizen expected: temples, forums, baths and an amphitheatre - which can still be traced.

The medieval period left us not only the Cathedral and the ornate Market Cross but the less well known St Mary's Hospital, built around 1290 and a rare example of a type which, incorporating a chapel and an infirmary under the one heavily-timbered roof, was once common all over Europe.

Several poets have connections with the city. William Collins, born here in 1721, has memorials in both the Cathedral and the church of St Andrew Oxmarket, north of East Street. John Keats took inspiration for the writing of The Eve of St Agnes from a visit to Chichester and nearby Stansted Park. William Blake, who thought Chichester 'a very handsome city', was tried for treason here (see The Sussex Story, p. 64) while living, courtesy of William Hayley, at Felpham.

THE CITY OF GOD

House prices in Chichester today are determined by the line of a wall put up by its citizens in the third century AD. A house inside this Roman wall, the circuit of which is still virtually complete, is worth double its equivalent outside. Asked why, the estate agents say that outside the wall: 'You feel that you are there, but you are not quite there. You're in Chichester, but you're not *in* Chichester.' It is the difference between the urbs and the suburbs, the thing itself and its accretions.

Adam Nicolson: 'Prospects of England'

I saw Chichester. It had simply never occurred to me before that day that towns could have a shape and be, like my beloved locomotives, things with character and meaning. If you had been drawing 'engines' for years and were then suddenly taken to such a city, you would instantly see what I mean. I had not been training myself to become an engineer. I had been training myself to see Chichester, the human city, the city of God, the place where life and work and things were all in one and all in harmony. The plan is clear and clean and rational - a thing of beauty having unity, proportion and clarity.

Eric Gill: 'Autobiography'

Chichester - Market Cross & Cathedral

• *Market Cross, Chichester*
197: SU 861048

• *Chichester Cathedral*
(01243) 782595
197: SU 859048

• *St Mary's Hospital*
Almshouses,
St Martin's Square
(01243) 783377
197: SU 862050

Tourist Information,
(01243) 775888

• *Site of Roman amphitheatre*
(west of Velyn Avenue)
197: SU 867046

Where John Keats began
The Eve of St Agnes:
• *11 Eastgate Square*
(private, with plaque)
197: SU 866045

Where William Blake was
tried for treason:
• *Guildhall Museum*
(01243) 784883)
197: SU 860048

Where William Blake lived:
• *Blake's Cottage,*
Blake's Road, Felpham
(private, with plaque)
197: SZ 951997

Nearby attractions:

• *Fishbourne Roman Palace*
(01243) 785859
197: SU 840052

• *Weald & Downland Open*
Air Museum, Singleton
(01243) 811348
197: SU 875128

• *Tangmere Military*
Aviation Museum
(01243) 775223
197: SU 906061

Where Eric Gill lived
in Sussex:
• *Sopers, High Street,*
Ditchling (private)
198: TQ 325153

The seaside resort was a fashionable eighteenth century invention. Before the new craze for healthy sea bathing, based on the success of urban spas, few houses of note were built to face the moody, hostile ocean. Today, by contrast, a retirement home with at least a glimpse of the sea is the dream of millions - and our Sussex coast has made a few hundred thousands of those dreams come true. It isn't, by and large, a glorious seaside - sand replaces shingle only some distance west of Brighton, and a bungaloid sprawl disfigures much of it - but the resort towns, great and small (Hastings, Bexhill, Eastbourne, Brighton, Worthing, Littlehampton and Bognor, to give the run of them east to west) each have their distinctive features and atmospheres. Stroll around spacious Eastbourne, that Queen of Watering Places 'built by gentlemen for gentlemen', with its enduring echoes of a grandeur imposed by the Duke of Devonshire, and you couldn't for a moment imagine you were in seedy, cheery, streetwise Brighton. Similarly, staidly tranquil Worthing seems more than a few dozen miles from seagull and artist haunted Hastings. Try them!

And then there are the cliffs: a warm honeycombed sandstone where the rocks of the High Weald meet the sea at Hastings, glistening white chalk from Eastbourne west to Brighton. From Beachy Head to Cuckmere Haven and up again to Seaford Head the Downs are safe from development, if not from erosion - the Seven Sisters a rare and stunning example of unspoiled coastal scenery.

FACING OUTWARDS

'Good old Sussex by the Sea': the words come from a popular parody, but the basic truth is undeniable. Sussex depends on its sea; and even though most of its visitors and an ever increasing number of its residents work in London, it is still facing outwards, away from the metropolis. And north Sussex is always looking south, to the line of the Downs which becomes a firmer guarantee of the sea beyond than an uninterrupted view could have been.

Ian Nairn: 'The Buildings of England - Sussex'

— Seven Sisters from Birling Gap —

- *The Seven Sisters
& Cuckmere Haven
199: TV 530970*

- *Seven Sisters Country
Park Centre, Exceat
(01323) 870280
199: TV 518996*

*Other attractions of the
Cuckmere Valley:*

- *The Living World
(01323) 870100
(at Country Park Centre)*

- *Alfriston Clergy House
(National Trust)
(01323) 870001
199: TQ 523029*

- *Drusillas Zoo Park,
near Alfriston
(01323) 870234
199: TQ 525049*

- *English Wine Centre
(next door to Drusillas)
(01323) 870164
199: TQ 525051*

- *Litlington Tea Gardens
(oldest in Sussex)
(01323) 870222
199: TQ 523018*

- *Michelham Priory,
Upper Dicker
(Sussex Archaeological
Society)
(01323) 844224
199: TQ 558093*

*See 'Sea-water Cures' in
The Sussex Story for the
development of seaside
resorts*

*See 'Sussex by the Sea' in
Living Sussex for a
selection of nature reserves
and rock pools*

CROOK AND BELL

If I had store,
By sheep and fold
I'd give you gold.
But since I'm poor,
By crook and bell
I wish you well

Shepherds' toast

Here is a world which has disappeared within living memory. For the naturalist W.H. Hudson, who began writing his Nature in Downland during 1899, it was impossible to imagine the Downs without the thousands of sheep whose constant cropping had produced the characteristic springy turf with its dense clusters of sweet-smelling herbs: 'The solitary shepherd with his dog at his feet will doubtless stand watching his flock on the hillside for some thousands of years to come.' But the economics of the countryside are changeable. The compact four-square Southdown perfected by John Ellman of Glynde a century earlier (and illustrated here) was still common in Hudson's time: today it's a rare breed, and some of the small flocks of sheep which persist on the Downs owe their existence not to hard-headed farmers but to naturalists anxious to preserve the threatened flora and fauna.

Shepherds, regarded with something close to reverence by many middle-class writers, no doubt tended towards the laconic, but we must suspect that the virtual dumbness recorded by Viscountess Wolseley was a reflection of her own reserve as much as theirs. Certainly the likes of Barclay Wills and Tickner Edwardes mixed with them easily enough: their accounts of life on the hills are both colourful and free of false piety. Maude Robinson, brought up in a Quaker family on a small farm north of Brighton during the 1860s, was similarly clear-eyed about the life, and she has left us a vivid account of a rural Sussex childhood.

Very near the earth the shepherd lives, growing up as her child, knowing all her secrets, never desiring to leave her. We heard of one who had lived seventy years in sight of the sea and never been on it, had never been in a train, and never out of Sussex. When he died they would put a lock of wool in his hands so that on Judgement Day the Recording Angel should know why he could not always be at church.

Arthur Mee: 'The King's England - Sussex'

One of the numerous, mostly minute, differences to be detected between the downland shepherd and other peasants - differences due to the conditions of his life - refers to his disposition. He has a singularly placid mind, and is perfectly contented with his humble lot. In no other place have I been in England, even in the remotest villages and hamlets, where the rustics are not found to be more or less infected with the modern curse or virus of restlessness and dissatisfaction with their life. I have, first and last, conversed with a great many shepherds, from the lad whose shepherding has just begun to the patriarch who has held a crook, and 'twitched his mantle blue' in the old Corydon way, on these hills for upwards of sixty years, and in this respect have found them all very much of one mind. It is as if living alone with nature on these heights, breathing this pure atmosphere, the contagion had not reached them, or else that their blood was proof against such a malady.

W.H.Hudson: 'Nature in Downland'

'I reckon I be reg'lar soft,'
He said to me; 'but theer,
I bin a nursemaid ev'ry spring
Fur nigh on seventy year!'

Barclay Wills: 'The Old Shepherd'

We shall be lucky if we can get talking with one of those weather-beaten shepherds who mind their flocks in solitude day after day and consequently almost lose the art of speech.

Viscountess Wolseley: 'Sussex in the Past'

Wherever one goes on the Sussex Downs today there is a new sound upon the air - the faint, shrill, yammering chorus from the lambing-pens. I came across one of these snug stockades this morning, and having found a gap in its high rampart of yellow straw, looked in awhile upon the busy scene.

Outside in the open down, the south-western gale was driving great grey cloud-shadow helter-skelter over the waste of sunlit green. But within the lambing-yard there was not breath enough to move a single straw in all the wide rectangle littered everywhere kneedeep as with golden fleece. In this soft warm carpet the gravid ewes were lying about luxuriously, waiting their turn to be allotted one of the little side-pens. The old shepherd was wandering down the long row of these cosy coupes walled and partially roofed by straw-plaited hurdles, and in almost every one he seemed to find something needing his attention. Descrying me at last, he shouted some words, wholly inaudible in the din. But coming over presently he was able to give me the tale of his luck so far. 'Nineteen: one for every day of the month,' said he, 'and ten of them all in the one gurt blowy night! 'Tis allers the wind that brings the lambs.'

Tickner Edwardes: 'A Downland Year'

I don't remember the vet coming out to the sheep. The shepherds always coped with any problems - we seldom lost a lamb. The tail docking and castration we did ourselves. We boys had to put on an old apron and hold the upturned lambs, one at a time, on our chests with a front and back leg held up together in one hand, the same with the other hand. Father came along with a very sharp knife, and with a quick flick cut their tail off! The other was taken off with a pair of pliers. They didn't bleed very much - just a bit. We put them down afterwards and they went running off. I can't remember losing any lambs through that, and they didn't dress them or anything. Some shepherds used to castrate the lambs by biting it off - I didn't fancy doing that!

Len Tuppen: 'Only Yesterday'

Sheepshearing day was one of the events of the year. If the weather was doubtful the flocks would be sheltered in the large barns the previous night. I have seen a most curious effect when the many hundreds of pairs of luminous eyes turned towards us in the darkness, the bodies of the sheep being quite invisible.

Maude Robinson: 'A South Down Farm in the Sixties'

• *Maude Robinson's farm, Saddlescombe*
198: TQ 273115

Where W.H. Hudson is buried:
• *Broadwater Cemetery*
198: TQ 143044

Where John Ellman is buried:
• *Glynde churchyard*
198: TQ 457093

Where to see spring lambing in Sussex:

• *Sussex Sheep Centre, Birling Farm, East Dean*
(01323) 423302
199: TV 558970

• *Church Farm, Coombes*
(01273) 452028
198: TQ 192081

See also 'A Weakly Lamb', p. 42

21

PICTURES TO MEMORY

Rivers attract a fierce loyalty from those who live by them, so it had better be explained that the Arun earns its selection here merely by virtue of being largest of the four which, rising in the Weald, cut through the chalk of the Downs to meet the sea - the Arun at Littlehampton, the Adur at Shoreham, the Ouse at Newhaven and the Cuckmere by the Seven Sisters at Cuckmere Haven (which, despite the bypassing of its famous meanders by a cut, is the only one to have avoided development as a port). Indeed, many a writer has plumped for a tributary of the Arun, the fast-flowing little Rother, as the choicest of them all: snaking across the Hampshire border at Durford (197: SU 774230), and skirting Midhurst on its way through sequestered fields and copses to meet the Arun near Pulborough, it flows under the ancient stone bridges of Trotton (built around 1300 by a member of the Camoys family) and Stopham (the very best in Sussex, rebuilt in 1423).

The upper reaches of the Arun once ran alongside the Wey & Arun Canal which, joining it at Pallingham Lock, connected the Sussex coast with the Thames. Lower down, the Arun winds through the tranquil watermeadows of the Amberley Wildbrooks before passing close to Amberley itself (p. 9) and running under the castle at Arundel (p. 56) - 'a district of the Downs so made,' as Belloc asserts with typical reserve in The Four Men, 'that when one sees it one knows at once that here is a jewel for which the whole county of Sussex was made.'

The Arun from the Black Rabbit to north of Burpham is the most beautiful stretch of river in Sussex.

George Aitchison: 'Sussex'

Sussex rivers are not noted for striking beauties - no gorges, rocks or waterfalls adorn them, and the waters of East Sussex are inclined to be muddy. But the Arun offers enchanting pictures to memory, running under overhanging beechwoods, or clear in the sunshine, or - perhaps most magical of all - as seen from the high bluff of Burpham, meandering along amid a thick embroidery of reeds and rushes and willow herb, with the romantic towers of Arundel Castle beyond.

Esther Meynell: 'Sussex'

R. Arun from Greatham Bridge

All we four stood upon that height in the rain that did not hide the lights upon the fields below and beyond us, and we saw white and glinting in the water-meadows the river Arun, which we had come so many miles to see; for that earlier happening of ours upon his rising place and his springs in the forest did not break our pilgrimage. Our business now was to see Arun in his strength, in that place where he is already full of the salt sea tide, and where he rolls so powerful a water under the Bridge and by Houghton Pit and all round by Stoke Woods and so to Arundel and to the sea. Then we looked at that river a little while, and blessed it, and felt each of us within and deeply the exaltation of return, the rain still falling on us as we went.

Hilaire Belloc: 'The Four Men'

I came down off the high summits, descending past the chalk pits to Houghton bridge against whose weathered buttresses the waters of Arun were swirling with the change of tide. I crossed the valley and behind me the river curved, so that it was now flowing by my side. Then I turned southwards, down the tow-path where the great hanging woods of Arundel come plunging down off the chalk summits to the edge of the winding river. Embedded in the crumbling soil were the trunks of trees so massive and immense that they seemed wrought of mildewed iron rather than of knotted wood. I stopped here for a while. The river was swiftly slipping through the rushes and across the valley the rim of the Downs was dropping slowly towards the coast. The sunlight caught its contours, the sage-green of the gorse bushes and the tawny patches of the harvested fields. I could see the little cluster of roofs which is Burpham and northwards the chalk pits of Houghton stood out like white shells against the hillside where I had first lingered.

Gerard Young: 'Come Into the Country'

You can cross the Arun in one of two places, either at Houghton over a stone bridge which carries the B2139 road, or by a footbridge at Bury. This would be my own choice. The bridge gives on to a path which takes you to Amberley over half a mile of the Amberley Wild Brooks. Personally, I cannot simply cross it. I look and I linger and the hours pass unnoticed. Streams, ditches, dykes and half-hidden pools mingle with pasture, sedge and reedbeds. Willows overhang the water. Wildfowl feed and nest among the runnels. The redshank's plaintive cry is never absent . On a sunny summer's day the heat beats up into your face from water and moist, wrinkled earth. The marsh vegetation is lush and verdant green, and some of the plants are rare. Under the north winds of winter the whole area turns brown and tawny, and if the cold deepens the resident wildfowl find they have company, which may include the beautiful goose-like Bewick's Swan from the Arctic.

Ben Darby: 'The South Downs'

• The Black Rabbit, Arundel
197: TQ 026085

Bridges over the Arun:

• Houghton Bridge
197: TQ 026118
• Bury footbridge
197: TQ 017130
• Greatham Bridge
197: TQ 032163

Medieval bridges over the western Rother:

• Trotton
197: SU 836224
• Stopham
197: TQ 030183

• Pallingham Lock
197: TQ 038214

Attractions close to the River Arun:

• Amberley Wildbrooks
197: TQ 030140

(see Amberley village, pp 8-9)

• Chalk Pits Industrial Museum
(01798) 831831
197: TQ 031123

• Bignor Roman Villa
(01798) 869259
197: SU 987147

• Parham House
(01903) 742021
197: TQ 060143

• Arundel Castle
(01903) 883136
197: TQ 018073

See 'Tails of the River Bank' in Living Sussex *for the wildlife of Sussex rivers*

See 'Goods by Water' in The Sussex Story *for canals and navigations*

23

Since the profile of Sussex resembles nothing so much as a heavy and immovable pig, it's fitting that the county's unofficial motto should be the squarely uncompromising Wunt Be Druv: someone should perhaps adapt Arthur Beckett's suggestion and create a suitably shaped badge with the stubborn message blazoned across it.

If it seems improbable that bloody-mindedness should once have characterised the whole Sussex race, we have to admit that there is plenty of evidence for it. Most writers, of course, have chosen to stress the positive aspects of this doggedness, (Kipling's 'hard-bitten South-country poacher' is also 'the best man-at-arms you can find'), and John Coker Egerton, a former rector of Burwash, is particularly entertaining - and never disdaining - in his accounts of the peculiar manners of the local people: the subtitle of his book, only a little tongue-in-cheek one imagines, is 'Stray Studies in the Wealden Formation of Human Nature'.

W.Victor Cook, who wrote several forgotten novels with Sussex settings, was a master of light verse and I wish there were room for more of it. His three stanzas on the native cussedness were published in 1950 when it must already have been largely a remembered trait. The exiled northern bishop 'Mus' (the dialect for Master) Wilfrid was himself a cantankerous individual, and therefore presumably had some sympathy with the boorish people to whom he brought Christianity (and, allegedly but incredibly, the art of fishing) at the end of the seventh century.

WUNT BE DRUV

When he stands like an ox in the furrow with his
sullen set eyes on your own,
And grumbles, 'This isn't fair dealing,' my son, leave
the Saxon alone.

Rudyard Kipling: 'Norman and Saxon'

My grandfather had a one-word reply to anyone who had the temerity to enquire when he would finish a job. Invariably, he would answer, 'Drackly' (directly), meaning not straight away but when he was good and ready.

Tony Wales: 'A Sussex Garland'

Much of this conservatism of character is no doubt due to his native obstinacy, for that trait of the Sussex peasant is proverbial, and it has been humorously suggested that his proper arms and motto would be the counterfeit presentment of a pig, with the words 'I wunt be druv!' inscribed thereon. But though your Sussex man will not be driven, it should be remarked that he may often be led, and fair persuasion will frequently win a way where argumentative tactics will leave him unmoved.

Arthur Beckett: 'The Spirit of the Downs'

Strangers who have bought property in the parish have often been greatly struck by the 'fore-rightness' and impatience of anything approaching to high-handed treatment exhibited by our working men. I well remember the conclusion to which a retired officer of the army soon came who had bought one of our farms, and who found that orders given in barrack-yard tone were not received with exactly barrack-yard submission. He honestly avowed that he would far sooner command a regiment of soldiers than one Burwash labourer.

Another new proprietor, who is long since dead, but whose temper and language while he was with us were not quite such as accorded with our views of what is due from an employer to those whom he employs, speedily received from one of his labourers the following assurance.

'You see, sir, it's like this. If you was to go on at me for about five minutes as you go on at your gardener, we should part.'

John Coker Egerton: 'Sussex Folk & Sussex Ways'

Besides stubbornness and phlegm, the Sussex character was marked by dogged independence and self-reliance together with a sturdy refusal to be impressed or over-awed by anybody or anything. The last trait may have come from there being so many small-holders and yeomen farmers, since Sussex was one of the few English counties where there really were peasants in the true sense of the word. Deep, ingrained reserve was accompanied by taciturnity and a dry, ironical and occasionally savage sense of humour.

Desmond Seward: 'Sussex'

a hand-bitten, South-country poacher.

Some folks as comes to Sussex,
They rackons as they knows
A darn sight better what to do
Than silly folk like me and you
Could possibly suppose.
But them as comes to Sussex
They mustn't push and shove,
For Sussex will be Sussex,
And Sussex won't be druv.

Mus' Wilfrid came to Selsey,
Us heaved a stone at he,
Because he rackoned he could teach
Our Sussex fishers how to reach
The fishes in the sea.
But when he dwelt among us,
Us gave un land and love,
For Sussex will be Sussex,
And Sussex won't be druv.

All folks as comes to Sussex
Must follow Sussex ways,
And when they've larned to know us well
There's no place else they'd wish to dwell
In all their blessed days.
There ant no place like Sussex
Until you goos Above,
But Sussex will be Sussex,
And Sussex won't be druv!

W. Victor Cook: 'Sussex Won't be Druv'

There's a brash side to Hastings - more accurately a brash eastern seafront - which is far from hidden and beautiful, but any visitor with time to explore is likely to fall under the salty spell of this varied, vigorous, somewhat ramshackle place. Many writers and artists have loved it, among them the poet Coventry Patmore and the Pre-Raphaelite Dante Gabriel Rossetti, who was married in St Clement's Church and lodged (there's a plaque) in High Street.

The historic Old Town lies between two great hills, with cliff railways climbing to the Norman castle on the western summit and to the unspoilt coastal scenery of Hastings Country Park on the eastern. In medieval times the twin parishes of All Saints and St Clement's lay either side of the Bourne stream: the road to Rye now marks its route, but the two ancient thoroughfares of All Saints Street and High Street retain some splendid old half-timbered buildings.

The town traditionally lived by the sea - it was the only Sussex member of the original Cinque Ports - and it has its fishermen still. Their boats are pulled up on the shingle of the Stade along the eastern foreshore, hard by their unique tall timbered storage sheds (the 'net shops') and a group of related attractions.

The last military defeat on home soil takes its name from Hastings because this was the nearest settlement of any size in 1066, but the Conqueror's victory was actually achieved on an uninhabited sandy ridge a few miles to the north-west. The town of Battle grew up alongside the abbey William built in celebration.

HIDDEN BEAUTIES

'Popular with visitors since 1066'

Hastings tourism slogan

I have never found anybody who didn't enjoy a visit to Hastings. It is wholly unpretentious. It puts on no airs even if it has few graces.

S.P.B. Mais: 'The Land of the Cinque Ports'

Hastings arouses strong likes and dislikes. Personally, I think that on a fine day in late autumn when the holiday season is over, the Old Town is one of the pleasantest places on the South Coast.

Desmond Seward: 'Sussex'

It runs up from the sea to one of the most thrilling heights of the Downs 600 feet up, and its ridge is crowned with the ruins of the Conqueror's castle. Stirring it is to walk about these broken walls, up stone steps worn by the feet of centuries, with all about us bits of ancient altars, broken arches, fragments of carved capitals, a holy water stone, and a pathetic remnant of the sedilia fading away on the walls. Here sat the priests by the altar, perhaps on one of those

great days when William Rufus summoned the bishops to pay him homage. Here stands the chancel arch set up 700 years ago, found 600 years later flat on the ground.

Arthur Mee: 'The King's England - Sussex'

This may not be the smartest, but it is arguably the most exciting, of the south-east coast resorts.

Oliver Mason: 'South-East England'

There is scarcely anything more striking and beautiful on the shores of the Mediterranean than the Old Town, seen on a bright day from the end of a pier or from a boat on the sea; and a gallery might be filled with the lovely aspects of it from the East Cliff and the Castle Hills.

Coventry Patmore: 'Old Hastings'

There is, of course, another side of the town which is frequented by the 'day-trippers' from London and nearby towns. You will find some of them at the amusement arcades and chip shops of the town. I am all for everyone enjoying their leisure moments in whatever takes their fancy. But it seems a great shame that so many of these hidden beauty spots still remain lost to the casual visitor.

James Meredith: 'Old Town Hastings - a Pictorial Guide'

• Hastings Castle
(01424) 717963
199: TQ 822094

• Sea Life Centre
(01424) 718776
199: TQ 827094

• Shipwreck Heritage Centre
(01424) 437452
199: TQ 827094

Tourist Information
(01424) 718888

• Battle Abbey and
1066 battlefield
(English Heritage)
(01424) 773792
199: TQ 748157

Where Coventry Patmore
lived in Hastings:
• Old Hastings House,
High Street (formerly
Mansion House; private)
199: TQ 826098

Fishermen's Beach, Hastings

AN AREA LEFT BEHIND

If you stand on the 670ft crest of Bow Hill and look south you will see spread out below a low and level land, and you will see nothing else like it in Sussex. The wide water and long inlets of Chichester Harbour thrust deep into the land, which is also patterned by the threads of innumerable streams and dykes. The sea shimmers beyond it. Over all the flat countryside soars the spire of Chichester Cathedral. This land is called the Sussex coastal plain.

Ben Darby: 'View of Sussex'

In spite of a dead flatness and generally deserted look, it possesses a fascination which grows on you as you get to know it better. Mr E.V. Lucas was surprised to find adders on the high roads. You will learn to be surprised at nothing. The whole area seems to have been left behind by the rest of England.

S.P.B. Mais: 'Sussex'

It looks at its best from a distance, for example from the windmill at Halnaker, or from the round barrows on Bow Hill above Kingley Vale, where the crowded roads and the packed houses lie in haze, the spire of Chichester Cathedral dwarfs the city, and the Isle of Wight looms behind the shining flats of Chichester Harbour. At closer range, one has to choose one's time and one's route with care, to find refuge beside the bird-haunted walls of Pagham Harbour.

Marcus Crouch: 'The Heritage of Sussex'

Coastal plain nr. Apuldram – looking towards Chichester

Geologically speaking, the coastal plain is quite separate from the rest of Sussex - a flat and fertile country once covered by a fickle come-and-go sea which today laps the ends of roads forlornly bound for settlements long lost beneath the waves. The old churchyard at Middleton, east of Bognor Regis, dramatically evoked in 1785 by that remarkable and prolific poet and novelist Charlotte Smith (who managed to support a large family from her pen after leaving a feckless husband), is now probably half a mile out to sea. The same fate befell St Wilfrid's minster at Selsey centuries ago.

The coastal strip between Shoreham and Chichester Harbour has some fine stretches of sand, and Bracklesham Bay is noted for its fossils, but it is for the most part fringed by a distinctly unappetising swathe of housing. It pays to strike out north into the flatlands below the A27, however. In the church at North Mundham, for instance, you'll find a large font fashioned from a single block of what is commonly known as Sussex marble - a grey-green sedimentary limestone, once extensively quarried in the Kirdford area (the font there is made of it, too) and comprising masses of compacted fossilised freshwater snails. At Eastergate a magnificent old granary with walls of half-timbered brick stands clear of the ground on mushroom-shaped staddle-stones. Between Hunston and Ford the course of the short-lived Portsmouth and Arun Canal (see <u>The Sussex Story</u>, p. 71) can still be traced across the fields.

Pressed by the Moon, mute arbitress of tides,
While the loud equinox its power combines,
The sea no more its swelling surge confines,
But o'er the shrinking land sublimely rides.
The wild blast, rising from the western cave,
Drives the huge billows from their heaving bed;
Tears from their grassy tombs the village dead,
And breaks the silent sabbath of the grave!

Charlotte Smith: 'Middleton: written
in the churchyard'

• *Chichester Cathedral*
(01243) 782595
197: SU 859048

• *Granary at Eastergate*
197: SU 945051

Sussex marble:
• *North Mundham church*
197: SU 875022

• *Kirdford church*
186/197: TQ 018265

Where Charlotte Smith
lived:
• *Woolbeding House,*
Woolbeding (private)
197: SU 872222

See also 'Creeks and
Dunes', p. 34

See <u>Living Sussex</u> *for*
migrating birds, marine
life and the wildlife of
shingle banks, sand dunes,
saltmarsh & mudflats,
wetlands & grazing marsh

He who is tired of the Sussex Downs, to adapt Dr Johnson, is tired of life. The range rises at Beachy Head and sweeps west into Hampshire, its northern scarp steep and shaded, its gentler southern flanks exposed to the warm sun and the sea breezes.

Kipling described these soft hills as whale-backed, but they have that famous rounded sleekness chiefly in his own part of Sussex, becoming more wooded towards the west where plantations spread across large feudal estates. No writer has thought to ignore them, and some have found themselves quite carried away. Revere them as we may, we surely hesitate to side with the great curate-naturalist Gilbert White in granting them mountain status. The otherwise rather prim and proper Arthur Beckett (a founder member of the Society of Sussex Downsmen and founder-editor of the late lamented Sussex County Magazine) cuts a comic figure as he bounds with a great shout across the springy turf to receive from the Spirit of his book's title 'the gift that makes a man master of the world', but no-one who has been up there can deny at least catching his drift. This is God's own countryside.

White, Thomas and Hudson all have reputations beyond Sussex for their nature writing. Galsworthy may seem the odd man out in this illustrious company, but the author of The Forsyte Saga lived under the Downs at Bury and after his death in 1933 his ashes were given 'in fee to the wind' (to quote another of his poems) on Bury Hill. His 'cardoon' is the dwarf thistle, Carduus nutans.

KINGDOM OF GRASS AND SKY

I've given my soul to the Southdown grass,
And sheep-bells tinkled where you pass.
Oh, Firle an' Ditchling an' sails at sea,
I reckon you keep my soul for me!

Rudyard Kipling: 'Puck of Pook's Hill'

The Downland air is always fresh and pure. It has a quality which elevates the spirits and braces the physical frame.

Arthur Beckett: 'The Spirit of the Downs'

A few years ago, at a small gathering of friends, someone posed the question, 'If you did not live in London, where would you best like to be?' I waited, listening to others pitching their tents in Hertfordshire, the Cotswolds, Dorset, Devon, even Suffolk. When my turn came, I answered without hesitation. 'I know exactly where I would choose. It would be on a south-facing slope two miles north of the South Downs, looking at them.'

I will not dwell here on the other advantages: one of England's warmest counties, and her sunniest, and the excellent train service to the metropolis. I am thinking now of the visual delights.

The gently billowing outline of the Downs suggests their structure: chalk, soft enough to have been shaped by aeons of wind and rain.

Alec Clifton-Taylor: 'Six More English Towns'

Though I have now travelled the Sussex Downs upwards of thirty years, yet I still investigate that chain of majestic mountains with fresh admiration year by year. There is something peculiarly sweet and amusing in the shapely-figured aspect of the chalk hills in preference to those of stone, which are rugged, broken, abrupt and shapeless. I never contemplate these mountains without thinking I perceive somewhat analogous to growth in their gentle swellings and smooth fungus-like protuberances, their fluted sides, and regular hollows and slopes, that carry at once the air of vegetative dilatation and expansion.

Gilbert White: 'The Sussex Downs'

Those green curves as soft and gentle as the breasts of a sleeping girl.

Anthony Armstrong: 'The Year at Margarets'

An uncertain path keeps to the highest ridge. The sides of the Downs are invaded by long stream-like gorse-sided coombes, of which the narrow floor is palest green grass. The highest points command much of earth, all of heaven. They are treeless, but occasionally the turf is over-arched by the hoops of a brier thicket, the new foliage pierced by upright dead grey grass. They are the haunt of the swift, the home of wheatear and lark and of whatsoever in the mind survives or is born in this pure kingdom of grass and sky.

Edward Thomas: 'The South Country'

Oh, the Downs high to the cool sky!
  And the feel of the sun-warmed moss;
And each cardoon, like a full moon,
  Fairy-spun of the thistle floss;
And the beech grove, and a wood-dove,
  And the trail where the shepherds pass;
And the lark's song, and the wind-song,
  And the scent of the parching grass!

John Galsworthy

The song of the lark is a continuous torrent of contrasted guttural and clear shrill sounds and trills, so rapidly emitted that the notes, so different in character, yet seem to interpenetrate or to overlap each other; and the effect on the ear is similar to that on the eye of sober or dull and brilliant colours mixed and running into one another in a confused pattern. The acutest note of all, a clear piercing sound like a cry several times repeated, is like a chance patch of brilliant colour occurring at intervals in the pattern.

W.H. Hudson: 'Nature in Downland'

Where Arthur Beckett is buried:
• Friston churchyard
199: TV 552982

Where John Galsworthy lived:
• Bury House, Bury (private)
197: TQ 011132

See also:
'Crook and Bell', p. 20
'Old Mother Goring', p. 55
'Land of Health', p. 70

See 'A Walk in Paradise' in <u>Living Sussex</u> *for downland wildlife*

The Sussex Downs nr. North Stoke

GOOD ALE, THOU ART MY DARLING

There's no reason to believe that drink was ever more of a problem - or, indeed, a pleasure - in Sussex than elsewhere, but sufficient has been written about it to demand that we should shoulder our way into the snug. The shade of Belloc will be there before us, of course, and we might be lucky enough to find the Copper family singing from the repertoire recorded by Bob's father, Jim (p. 12). We shall no longer be able to quaff Gooche's Hailsham beer or the Old Stingo of Thomas Tipper, whose Newhaven tombstone urges us to 'be better, wiser; laugh more if you can', but the Harvey's brew is still being mashed at Lewes after two hundred years, and in more hygienic conditions: when contamination of the local water supply caused a typhoid epidemic in 1875 the head brewer reported that a 'filthy scum' had to be skimmed off each day, though 'of course we used it in brewing, purifying it by boiling, fermenting etc., turning out a pure beer.'

The diary of Thomas Turner - an East Hoathly shopkeeper, schoolmaster, undertaker, churchwarden and overseer of the poor - should be on every Sussex bookshelf for its glimpses of Sussex rural life in the eighteenth century. As these extracts from 1756 reveal, Turner was a regular sparring partner of the demon drink, and usually came off worst. Bumboo was a mixture of rum, sugar, water and nutmeg.

Since The Swan at Lower Fittleworth is a favourite, if occasional, haunt of mine, I'm delighted to note that E.V. Lucas declared it 'the most ingeniously placed inn in the world'. Cheers!

On Sussex hills where I was bred,
When lanes in autumn rains are red,
When Arun tumbles in his bed,
　And busy great gusts go by;
When branch is bare in Burton Glen
And Bury Hill is a whitening, then
I drink strong ale with gentlemen;
　Which nobody can deny, deny,
　　Deny, deny, deny, deny,
　　Which nobody can deny!

Hilaire Belloc: 'The Four Men'

Tues 27 Jan: I came home again in liquor, but got home very well; though to do myself justice, I believe I was not extreme good humoured when I got home, and I do think I am prodigiously silly and apish when I am in liquor, having always, for a great while after, a sting of conscience for the same. I will, however, renew my former resolution and use my utmost endeavour to keep it; that is, not to get DRUNK again if I can avoid it.

Thomas Turner's Diary

There is no sin which doth more deface God's image than drunkenness: it disguiseth a person and doth even unman him. Drunkenness makes him have the throat of a fish, the belly of a swine and the head of an ass. Drunkenness is the shame of nature, the extinguisher of reason, the shipwreck of chastity and the murderer of conscience. Drunkenness is hurtful to the body, the cup kills more than the cannon, it causes dropsies, catarrhs, apoplexies, it fills the eye with fire and the legs with water and turns the body into an hospital.

Plaque on a wall at Kirdford

O Gooche's Beer your heart will cheer
　And put you in condition;
The man that will but drink his fill
　Has need of no physician:

'Twill fill your veins, and warm your brains
　And drive out melancholy;
Your nerves 'twill brace, and paint your face,
　And make you fat and jolly.

John Hollamby: 'Gooche's Beer'

Sun 28 Mar: We smoked a pipe or two and then went down to Jones's, where we drank one bowl of punch and two mugs of bumboo; Mr Ormeroid went away after the punch. I spent 12d and came home again in liquor. Oh with what horrors does it fill my breast to think I should be guilty of doing so - and on a Sunday, too. Let me once more endeavour never, no never, to be guilty of the same again. I am certain it proceeds, not from the love of liquor, but from a too easy temper and want of resolution.

Thomas Turner's Diary

It's you that makes my friends my foes,
It's you that makes me wear old clothes,
But since you come so near my nose
It's up you comes and down you goes!
O, good ale, thou art my darling,
Thou art my joy both night and morning.

Jim Copper's Song Book

A bad job. Pipes broken again. Obliged to brew from the river water. First brewing today very thick and muddy.

John Harvey's brewing journal, Lewes, 1833

Tues 8 June: What I am a-going to mention makes me shudder with horror at the thought of it. It is I got very much in liquor. But let me not give it so easy a name, but say I was very drunk, and then I must of consequence be no better than a beast. Oh! may the Supreme Director of all events give me grace to be wiser for the future.

Thomas Turner's Diary

• *The Swan,*
Lower Fittleworth
197: TQ 010185

• *Thomas Turner's house,*
East Hoathly
(private, with plaque)
199: TQ 522163

• *Kirdford plaque*
(Outside Trerose Cottage,
near the church)
186/197: TQ 018266

Sussex breweries
(tours by arrangement):

• *Harvey & Sons,*
Cliffe High Street, Lewes
(01273) 480209
198: TQ 419103

• *King & Barnes,*
Bishopric, Horsham
(01403) 270470
187: TQ 168307

The Swan - Fittleworth

CREEKS AND DUNES

Considering its size, Chichester Harbour is extraordinarily elusive. You do not see it from afar unless you are on the Downs, and you reach its banks abruptly and in great surprise. You then quickly discover that the word 'harbour' is more a comprehensive term for a district than for a place where ships tie up. The name itself can be confusing, for Chichester is two miles from the nearest wide water, though Chichester Channel pierces almost up to the city. But the name is of little consequence. The important thing is the place, which is beautiful, rich in wild life, particularly sea birds and waders, and is of vital historical and archaeological significance. It has also been designated an Area of Outstanding Natural Beauty. It is about eight miles broad and five miles long and it is an enchanting world of open water, winding creeks, sand dunes, and extensive saltings and mud flats.

Ben Darby: 'View of Sussex'

West Itchenor, where Charles II kept a yacht, has always earned its living from the sea and today it's the headquarters of the Chichester Harbour Conservancy, responsible for seventeen miles of navigable creeks and channels with moorings for some eight thousand pleasure boats. That scarcely credible figure explains why there are upwards of a dozen sailing clubs in the harbour. A ferry crosses the Chichester Channel from Itchenor in the summer months, the main attraction on the other side being Bosham - which you pronounce 'Bozzm' and which, for understandable reasons, has attracted legends about King Canute, none of which is likely to be true. Never mind: it's a lovely waterside spot, with a Saxon church that appears, for propaganda reasons, on the Bayeux Tapestry. (For more on this, and on the Roman connection with nearby Fishbourne, see The Sussex Story*). That link with Normandy was to be re-established - though the roles were reversed - during the last war, when sections of the Mulberry Harbour for the D Day landings were fabricated at Bosham, while minesweepers were built at Itchenor.*

The birdlife of Chichester and Pagham Harbours is remarkable (ten per cent of the world's population of dark-bellied brent geese overwinter here, for instance), but the fragile sand dunes of East Head are if anything even more highly valued by conservationists. 'They represent,' claims a Conservancy booklet, 'the nearest to a remaining natural habitat within the British Isles.'

— East Head —

At high water Bosham is beautiful. Boats bob at anchor or sail about the bay - it is a scene that has inspired many a contributor to the Royal Academy summer exhibitions. The only people not to appreciate it are the unfortunates who, like Canute, make a miscalculation about the tide and return to find the cars they had parked on dry land are over their wheels in water.

Brigid Chapman: 'Sussex - A Portrait in Colour'

At West Wittering is the 110-acre sand and shingle spit of East Head, east of the entrance to Chichester Harbour. Vulnerable to the constant battering it receives from the sea and, indeed, from the feet of visitors, East Head is important because it demonstrates how the sea has shaped this part of the coastline, and because it supports a variety of wildlife. The Trust has fenced off part of the spit, while marram grass is encouraged to 'bind' the dunes; naturalists come to see the waders, the plant and marine life, and the insect population.

National Trust Handbook

• *Chichester Harbour Conservancy, Itchenor (01243) 512301 197: SU 799014*

• *East Head (National Trust) 197: SZ 766990*

• *Bosham Church 197: SU 804039*

• *Pagham Harbour Local Nature Reserve (visitor centre) 197: SZ 857965*

See also 'An Area Left Behind', p. 28

See 'Fashioned by Wave & Wind' in <u>Living Sussex</u> *for the wildlife of sand dunes*

THE SMALLEST CHURCH IN ENGLAND

We turned left into the lane and clambered up to the top where there was a great field of corn growing. And a little path waggling through it. And in the middle of the field, with great, huge trees all round it, was the Smallest Church in Sussex. Our house was the rectory. But all we had to do was change the water and the flowers in the vases once or twice a week. On the altar. Well, they weren't *vases* for the flowers. Jam jars. But we put white and blue crepe paper round them so they looked rather pretty. And my sister always picked the flowers and arranged them herself. Sitting in the sun on a gravestone singing a hymn-sounding-song.

There was a little wooden fence all round the church, with a squeaky iron gate and inside the gate was the churchyard. All the tombs and gravestones were squinty, like people standing on a ship in a storm. Leaning in all directions and covered with moss. There was no one buried there who was new. The newest one was called Anne Stacie Departed This Life 1778 aged 78. We thought that was very interesting but Angelica didn't. The door was always open and inside there was a lovely cool feeling and a smell of floor polish and candles. It was very, very small.

Sometimes the Rector, Mr Eric Bentley, came up and preached a sermon. One Sunday in the month. And we all went. And there was another for the Harvest. And then lots of people came with sheaves of corn and apples and bread and things. And it was lovely. Usually there were only about twelve or fifteen people there: it only had room for twenty anyway. And hikers used to come and people from as far away as Lewes and Polegate. It was too small inside for an organ so there was just a piano at the back and Winnie Maltravers playing hymns and singing very loudly. Shaking her bun, so that we waited for it to start falling down round her shoulders, which it always did - in long grey wisps like a horse's tail.

On these days Lally wore her Best Brown and a hat with ivy leaves on it which she bought one day in Seaford. It was a bit like a pudding basin and came right down to her eyes so that she had to tilt her head backwards to read the hymn book...only she never wore glasses so she just sang 'la la la la' all the time, pretending she could see the tiny printing. Which, of course, with that hat, she couldn't.

Our mother gave us a penny each for the collection when it came round during 'The Lord is My Shepherd'; and it was interesting to see how much was in the plate to send to the African Orphans somewhere. Never very much. Because the hikers were a poor looking lot and no one ever gave more than a sixpence or a threepenny-bit. But Mr Bentley sent it all off to Africa once a month or so, with the collection from his big church in the village.

'This is the smallest church in England,' said my sister, 'and that's the altar where the murder was.'

Dirk Bogarde: 'A Postillion Struck by Lightning'

• *Lullington Church*
(with the rectory next door)
199: TQ 528031

The church - Lullington

There are, of course, those
who dislike Brighton, but
usually for the very reasons
others love it - the bustle,
the wide-boy raffishness, the
hint of licentiousness.
Actors and journalists are
notoriously attracted to it.
The aura of dirty weekends
glows dingily about it even
though the phrase itself
seems quaintly out-of-date.
It was the first place I ever
saw men holding hands in
the street. Graham Greene,
with his nose for the rancid,
found ample material for his
Thirties tale of race gangs
and protection racketeers.
John Arlott, better known
as a cricket commentator
than a poet, clearly found
seediness to his liking, too.

Brighton, then, is set
apart from every other town
in Sussex, though Hastings
might rival its raciness if
only it were closer to
London. Even its town hall
politics are distinctive: a
rare Labour enclave (another
is Crawley) in a county
predominantly Conservative
and, by steady increase,
Liberal Democrat. Its
working class traditions are
honoured -'It was,' he tells
us, 'a beautiful world' - in
the autobiography of the
self-taught A.E. Coppard,
brought up in late Victorian
Brighton. (His growlers
were drivers of four-wheeled
cabs; the Chain Pier was
wrecked by a storm in 1896).

Brighton remains a place
to live in. Let trippers flock
to the Palace Pier (pictured
here) and the pebbles, to
Volk's Railway and
Prinnie's Royal Pavilion,
the locals will relish their
secret: that areas such as
Kemp Town and North
Laine (below the station,
and not to be confused with
the touristy Lanes) are real
and vibrant communities,
villages within the town.

LONDON-BY-THE-SEA

Brighton! The very name conjures images of happy holidaymakers, cosmopolitan high life and outstanding architecture.

Timothy Carder: 'The Encyclopaedia of Brighton'

Brighton never lost its racy image, and a weekend there still has vastly different connotations to a weekend at Budleigh Salterton; or indeed Hove, which plays Jekyll to Brighton's Hyde.

Jim Cleland: 'The Visitor's Guide to Sussex'

It is London-by-the-sea; the mecca of the day-tripper; a source of endless wonder for the sociologist, the students of architecture and rude postcards, the artist and the historian; home for many famous actors; the inspiration of the novelist; in short, a place of almost limitless variety.

Michael H.C. Baker: 'Sussex Scenes'

They came in by train from Victoria every five minutes, rocked down Queen's Road standing on the tops of the little local trams, stepped off in bewildered multitudes into fresh and glittering air; the new silver paint sparkled on the piers, the cream houses ran away into the west like a pale Victorian water-colour; a race in miniature motors, a band playing, flower gardens in bloom below the front, an aeroplane advertising something for the health in pale vanishing clouds across the sky.

Graham Greene: 'Brighton Rock'

> All electric, down from London
> Every hour the green trains run,
> Bearing tribes of worshippers
> To the doubtful Brighton sun.
>
> Kipling has sung of the Sussex Downs
> And Belloc of Wealden beer,
> But I would tell a different tale,
> Of a doomed and garnished pier.
>
> Of an elegant Adam fireplace
> In a third-rate dancing club,
> Forgotten print of the Regent
> In a dusty, smoke-fumed pub.

John Arlott: 'Brighton'

In that paradise of brightness, the classic Brighton front with its grand hotels and shops, its bath-chairs perambulating fat old gentlemen, growlers waiting amiably for a fare, and goat-chaises with aristocratic children attached to spades and shrimping nets, radiated in a vast sparkle of never-ending sunlight from Hove to the Old Chain Pier.

A.E. Coppard: 'It's Me, O Lord!'

Anyone who does not live in Brighton must be mad and ought to be locked up.

S.P.B. Mais

• Palace Pier, Brighton
198: TQ 313035

Some other attractions in Brighton and Hove:

• Royal Pavilion, Old Steine
(01273) 603005
198: TQ 313042
(See 'Upturned Turnips' in <u>The Sussex Story</u>)

• Aquarium (now Sea Life Centre), opposite the pier
(01273) 604234
198: TQ 314039

• Volk's Railway
(from the pier to Brighton Marina)
198: TQ 315036

• Preston Manor
(01273) 603005
198: TQ 304063

• British Engineerium Nevill Road, Hove
(01273) 559583
198: TQ 286066

Tourist Information, Brighton
(01273) 323755

Other Sussex piers, west to east:

• Bognor Regis (disused)
197: SZ 935987

• Worthing
198: TQ 150023

• West Pier, Brighton (Grade I listed; disused)
198: TQ 303038

• Eastbourne
199: TV 619988

• Hastings
199: TQ 812089

The relentless, kaleidoscopic entanglements of the Bloomsbury Group are embodied both figuratively and literally in Angelica Garnett, who thought herself the daughter of the writer Clive Bell (and reasonably, since he was married to her mother, Vanessa Bell); who learned at the age of seventeen that her true father was Vanessa's fellow artist at Charleston, Duncan Grant ('Between Clive and Duncan there was not the faintest shadow of jealousy - indeed it seems absurd to mention such a thing'); and who lost her virginity ('appropriately enough, in H.G. Wells's spare bedroom') to a man who had been her father's lover.

If it is seductively easy to ridicule such complications, her autobiography forbids us. Angelica was an artist rather than a writer - a painting of hers on a bedroom door at Charleston is to my untrained eye one of the best things to be seen there - but this beautifully written memoir is infused with a mixture of sadness, delight and hard-won understanding.

Sussex is rich in Bloomsbury associations. At one time or another most of that colourful set of artists and intellectuals - Strachey, Forster, Fry & Co. - came to visit Vanessa at Charleston or her sister, the novelist Virginia Woolf, at nearby Rodmell. At Berwick Church, which had been damaged by a German bomb, Vanessa and Duncan were commissioned by the unrelated George Bell - Bishop of Chichester and patron of the arts - to paint the walls. Look out for local views, and for a Sussex trug basket in the Nativity scene.

BLOOMSBURY OCCASIONS

Once every fortnight in summer we would bundle into the car and, in the chalky stillness of a Sussex afternoon, drive over to Rodmell, crossing the Ouse at Southease level-crossing. Monk's House, in the heart of the village, was, very largely for this reason, as different from Charleston as possible. The house was long and narrow: the rooms opened out of each other in succession, the whole house lower than the garden outside, so that one stepped into it rather as one steps into a boat. Plants and creepers knocked at the small-paned windows as though longing to come in, invited perhaps by the green walls. Cool and peaceful, on a hot summer's day the house seemed to bubble gently, like a sun-warmed stone that has been dropped into a pool. As a little girl I had sometimes stayed at Monk's House as a guest, and once my cousin Judith and I had discovered the amusement of rolling down the steep lawn opposite the front door, only to be scolded by our nurses because we were bright green all over. Green is the colour that comes to mind when I think of the house and garden, with its curling fig trees and level expanse of lawn overlooking the water-meadows. Green was Virginia's colour; a green crystal pear stood always on the table in the sitting-room, symbol of her personality.

For tea we sat at the long table in the dining-room, the only big room there was. Virginia, sitting at one end, poured out tea, not as Vanessa did, with a careful, steady hand, but waving the teapot to and fro as she talked, to emphasise her meaning. Our cup and saucers were of delicate china, our food less solid than at Charleston - there were biscuits instead of cake, farmhouse butter procured by Virginia herself, and penny buns. Virginia ate little, popping small pieces of food into her mouth like a greyhound. Before tea was over she would light a cigarette in a long holder, and as her conversation took fire, she herself grew hazier behind the mounting puffs of smoke.

When the meal was over we all trooped into the garden, invited by Leonard to play the ritual game of bowls. If the first half of the entertainment had been Virginia's, the second was his. He took

charge of the game, pressing everyone to play, even the least experienced, who were given handicaps and praised if they did better than expected.

Meanwhile Virginia sat in a deckchair under the elm tree, smoking, talking to Vanessa about cousins seen again after many years, and laughing about them in their own quiet, throwaway fashion, like two birds on a perch. Alternatively, Virginia, unable to tolerate boredom, did her best to inspire rivalry between Charleston and Rodmell, preferring to squabble about houses rather than remain silent. Vanessa hated the thought of life in a village, and, albeit reluctantly, defended the liberty and privacy of Charleston, where we were a law unto ourselves, where no Mrs Ebbs looked over the garden wall or called out to one on one's way up the village street, and where there were no church bells to intrude on one's Sunday afternoon. But when I went to sit beside them Virginia would insist on trying to make me say that Rodmell was the superior of the two. In the end I would become impatient and she would say, 'Oh! Pixerina, what a devil you are! But you do love me, don't you?'

'Of course I do, Witcherina, but I can't lie to you.'

Angelica Garnett: 'Deceived With Kindness'

The Garden - Monk's House, Rodmell

- *Monk's House, Rodmell (National Trust) (01892) 890651 198: TQ 421064*

- *Charleston Farmhouse (Charleston Trust) (01323) 811265 199: TQ 493068*

- *Berwick Church (wall paintings) 199: TQ 519049*

Where Vanessa Bell and Duncan Grant are buried:

- *Firle churchyard 198: TQ 471072*

Houses (all private) with Bloomsbury associations:

- *Little Talland House, Firle (now Talland House: the Woolfs' first Sussex home, rented for a few months in 1911 before they moved to Asham House) 198: TQ 469073*

- *Site of Asham House 198: TQ 440062 (the house, which had been swallowed by a landfill site, was demolished in 1995)*

- *The Round House, Pipe Passage, Lewes (former windmill bought by the Woolfs in 1919, but promptly sold before the move to Monk's House) 198: TQ 409102*

- *Upper Tilton Farmhouse, near Charleston (John Maynard Keynes' country home) 199: TQ 495067*

A man who shook off the dull cares of a tobacconist's business for the pleasures of communing with shepherds might be imagined as a fanciful dreamer, but Barclay Wills kept his wits, and his wit, about him up on the hills and returned to record his experiences with careful detail. Shaun Payne, who has co-edited an excellent selection from three of Wills's books under the title The Downland Shepherds, finds the last of them, Shepherds of Sussex, 'the most authoritative work in the literature of shepherding and one of the finest rural books of our century.' Wills wrote it (in 1938) just in time: 'I had predicted the fading out of the old men, but it started sooner than I expected, so that although the book was begun as an up-to-date record it has already become the history of a race that has almost disappeared.'

Shepherds of Sussex is dedicated to Nelson Coppard, born at Poynings in 1863 and the first of that 'race' Wills knew: 'To the lucky natives of Sussex a meeting with a shepherd is just an ordinary incident in a Downland ramble, but to a Londoner, blessed with an artistic temperament, that first sudden entry into a little valley full of sheep with their ancient bells chiming, the meeting with a jovial shepherd with his glittering crook, the chat with him, and the return journey, when I carried home wild flowers and two large canister bells, was overwhelming. I felt that I had stepped into a new world.'

The 'pollard' in the bag is glossed in Parish's dialect dictionary as 'the refuse siftings of flour'.

A WEAKLY LAMB

My friend the shepherd had arranged his sheep-fold in a little hollow among the hills of Falmer, and thither I trudged to spend a few hours with him and to share, as far as possible, the duties of the day.

As 'shepherd's mate' I am afraid I was like the shepherd boy in Wordworth's poem - something between a hindrance and a help - but I accepted my friend's invitation to extend my visit and spend the night with him.

Without the sunshine of the previous day the north-east wind seemed doubly keen. A weakly lamb had arrived during the afternoon. 'Reckon it must be fed,' observed the shepherd, 'or it'll be a deader,' so after making all secure we walked to the farm, about half a mile away. Luckily there had been no bottle babies during the first week, but now this little extra duty had begun.

It was an easy walk over the soft Downland turf. The hills gradually faded. Masses of furze became dark, mysterious lumps of shadow, which swallowed up the dog as he hunted in vain for skulking rabbits. At length the farm loomed up in front of us and it was not long before I had shouldered a basket containing bottles of milk and some provisions, the shepherd carrying other tackle. Our return journey was made by moonlight. As we neared the gate leading towards the fold we turned off past the badger's home and cut across under the beeches with uncertain steps, for the black shadows of the branches chopped up the ground into all sorts of shapes, which appeared like roots and holes, so that it was almost a relief to step away from the queer zig-zag pattern and enter the valley where the flock lay.

Inside the shepherd's hut the little stove gave out a welcome warmth, for there was a touch of frost in the air. The milk was soon warmed and bottled, and the weak baby recovered amazingly as the magic warm fluid was sucked down.

Back to the hut we went and I was shown the two kinds of teats for the milk bottle - a modern one of rubber, and an old pattern as used by the shepherd's father - a cork with a groove at the side which held a pipe of elder twig bound in with rag. From the window we looked down on the hundred and thirty-seven waiting ewes in the big pen outside, all lying contentedly among the straw litter.

For the first few hours the moonlight was bright, and one felt that the lantern was hardly necessary for our visits in the fold. As we made our tours of inspection many of the ewes rose or moved and the bells rang loudly in the still night air. All the lambs there were born to the sound of the sheep bells.

The old man has a whimsical humour which never fails. He affected to treat me as a shepherd boy. 'Now, boy,' he said, 'hold thet light steady, can't ye, an' doan't jig 'un 'bout, or they ewes'll be froughten.' I obeyed meekly and got my reward. 'Hap I'll make a shepherd of ye yet!' he said; 'put thet kettle on if ye want to, for it be turnin' colder.' As we sipped our tea we still heard an occasional rattle from a 'cluck' bell, or the loud tinkle from the one 'latten' bell, and once, a low growl from the dog on guard outside.

We snatched an hour's sleep and woke at three o'clock. The moonlight was gone and only the stars kept vigil. Fortunately the piercing north-east wind had dropped a little, for we had to spend some time with a ewe before her baby arrived. Two more were found and moved to pens.

Four o'clock came. The shepherd was asleep on a bag of pollard, while I sat on another and wrote my notes by lantern light. At four-thirty he awoke. With mock solemnity he twitted me. Had I been round the fold? No! Had I put milk on to warm? No! Then what was the use of a mate at all? On went our coats again and we made the round - an easy tour this time, just one more baby, strong and well. My friend took the lantern and went for the milk, and once more I feasted my eyes on the scene, for the old horn-windowed lantern is a thing of beauty when in use. I stood behind and watched the shepherd simply for my own pleasure, for as the big, cloaked figure ascended the wooden steps of the hut I saw some fanciful resemblance to the figure of Father Christmas. Soon he returned and once more the mellow, pale orange light flickered over the dusky forms on the straw as we fed the weakly baby again.

Five o'clock at last! No need for the lantern in the fold now, for the light of dawn was changing the sky. 'Tis brakfus' time,' said the shepherd. So I went outside to fill our kettle from the churn and I did the job quickly, for the wind was back again and a thin coat of frost had appeared on the grass, the straw, and the wool of the resting sheep.

Two hours' work after breakfast was very welcome. Pens were rearranged and cleaned, the ewes were let out for a stretch and a feed and the fold tidied. The ice in the water trough was broken and fresh water pumped in. A quick inspection of the ewes and babies on the hillside was made and the count found to be correct. I was mildly surprised when the shepherd said 'Reckon 'tis brakfus' time,' but found this to be part of the usual routine. So on went the old kettle once more and, after a quick cold wash in a bucket, we again had breakfast. Crocks were cleaned, the hut swept, the fire raked out, and the day's round began again. We drove nearly a hundred and thirty ewes to the dewpond and back. Many were called to order by name. 'Granny' was last of all. She could not hurry. The shepherd has a soft spot for poor 'Granny'. His advice had been disregarded and she was not killed. Now the poor barren ewe, often ailing, plods along after the rest.

Barclay Wills: 'Bypaths in Downland'

• *Pyecombe Church (with 'Pyecombe crook' on centrally pivoting Sussex 'tapsell' gate) 198: TQ 292126*

Where Nelson Coppard was shepherd:
• *Mary Farm, Falmer (now St Mary's Farm) 198: TQ 348108*

Shepherds' bells and other Barclay Wills memorabilia :
• *Worthing Museum & Art Gallery, Chapel Road (01903) 239999 198: TQ 147030*

• *Where Barclay Wills's ashes were scattered:*
• *Woodvale Crematorium, Brighton 198: TQ 328057*

See 'Crook and Bell', p. 20

Pyecombe Church

There are poems a-plenty to the Downs and the Weald, but who sings of the Lower Greensand? It may be a negligible feature in the east of the county (though a tell-tale green tinge can be seen in the walls of Pevensey Castle and St Mary's Church in the Old Town at Eastbourne), yet it has bequeathed us not only the wonderful sandy commons of the Petworth/Midhurst region, but a lofty ridge which rises to all of 919 ft at Black Down - the highest point in Sussex, five hundred acres of it owned by the National Trust.

Tennyson's first, brief experience of living in Sussex had been a disaster (he and his pregnant wife moved into an isolated farmhouse at Warninglid in 1850 and fled when a storm demolished their bedroom wall), but he was to have better luck with Aldworth, the mansion that he built here nearly twenty years later and where he was to write Tiresias, many of his Arthurian poems and Rizpah - a monologue set, rarely for him, in Sussex. The piped hot water supply was such a luxurious novelty that the delighted laureate at first took several baths a day.

He died at Aldworth in October 1892, having asked for the blinds to be raised: 'I want to see the sky and the light.' A few days later, in the late afternoon, his coffin was borne away on a wagon down the hill to Lurgashall. 'Ourselves, the villagers and the schoolchildren followed over the moor towards a glorious sunset,' recalled his son Hallam, 'and later through Haslemere under brilliant starlight to Westminster Abbey.'

TENNYSON'S EYRIE

You came, and look'd and loved the view
Long known and loved by me,
Green Sussex fading into blue
* With one grey glimpse of sea.*

Alfred, Lord Tennyson: lines to a friend

I have never seen the earth flung about in such a wild way as round about Hindhead and Black Down.

William Cobbett: 'Rural Rides'

Black Down is a great wild plateau, a wilderness of heather, gorse and bracken, rising grandly through thick belts of woodland that clothe it in places to its very summit. Approach Black Down from the south, by way of Lodsworth and Lurgashall. Crossing the wide spaces of the common, you see the green heights towering above you as do the lower reaches of the Alps.

George Aitchison: 'Sussex'

The woods grow thicker as you climb, closing you in, but with tantalising glimpses of farms and fields far below. Then the woods thin out and suddenly you are on the brow of the hill, 919ft above

— Black Down —

sea-level, and the dappled beauty of the Weald stretches far away, far below, with a glimpse of silver sea through the Arun gap. This is one of the finest views in all the Weald. It is not the most expansive. Leith Hill can claim the widest prospect. But there is something subtly different about the view from Black Down, satisfying but strangely apart, and that is more to do, I think, with the hill itself than with the view. Leith Hill welcomes. Black Down keeps itself to itself. You feel not exactly an intruder but a tolerated visitor.

The sensation becomes marked when you find yourself not on a crest or a curved summit but on a wide, airy and heather-covered plateau. It is almost a primeval landscape. The heather is long, tough and tangled, and plentifully mingled with gorse; you may all too easily fall headlong into steep and unseen declivities. I have forced my way from one side to the other of this wild land and it is a tiring and dusty business. The prospects from the edge of the plateau are magnificent.

Ben Darby: 'Journey Through the Weald'

Where Tennyson lived:
• *Aldworth House, Black Down (private)*
186: SU 926309

Where Tennyson worshipped:
• *Lurgashall Church (with commemorative lectern)*
186/197: SU 938273

See 'The Teeming Greensand' in Living Sussex *for the wildlife of the western heaths*

1809 —Tennyson— 1892

They burn the Pope in Lewes every November the Fifth, a blazing night of misrule whose outlandish Protestant traditions (including the ferocious rantings of mock clerics to a background of fireworks and flames) spring not from the bloodletting of Queen Mary or the treachery of Guy Fawkes but from the bigotry of the nineteenth century. The martyrs memorial unveiled above Lewes in 1901 (nearly 350 years after those terrible burnings outside the Star Inn) was regarded by many at the time as a slap in the face for the town's Roman Catholics - and no wonder, since a fear that the 'smells and bells' ritualism of the Oxford Movement heralded an inexorable drift towards Rome had long occasioned attacks, physical as well as verbal, upon Catholics and High Anglicans alike.

Today, the religious rancour gone, we can enjoy this gaudy, cacophonous, acrid-smelling event for what it is, the greatest Bonfire Night in all England. Down the High Street marches, sways, explodes the Grand United Procession - two thousand celebrants in spectacular dress (Zulus, Aztecs, Vikings, Mexican caballeros); a forest of banners and effigies; the overlapping music of a dozen bands; the trundling of tar barrels with their cargoes of smouldering torches; a phalanx of burning crosses whose heat the spectator feels even through a closed window. Later, at their separate sites, the vivid firework displays organised by the five Lewes societies. Finally, around midnight, Last Post at the war memorial. There is, truly, nothing like it.

A PENNY LOAF TO FEED OLD POPE

Shortly before five o'clock we found ourselves in the principal street of the ancient town, bustling with people, protected by patrols of police, and resounding with the blows of hammers as carpenters boarded up doorways and windows, and covered in area gratings. All business had ceased; the front of both the County Hall and Town Hall was closely covered with wooden hoardings; the windows of the White Hart Hotel were guarded with wire blinds; while those of shops, public buildings and private houses were barricaded with deal boards or special shutters, as if for a siege, this precaution being necessary for protection against the Bonfire Boys' inherent practice of throwing fireworks in all directions.

Arthur Beckett: 'The Spirit of the Downs'

Remember, remember the fifth of November,
The gunpowder treason and plot.
I see no reason why gunpowder treason
Should ever be forgot.
Guy Fawkes, Guy Fawkes, he's intent
To blow up the King and Parliament:
Three score barrels of powder below
Poor old England to overthrow.
By God's providence he was catched
With a dark lantern and burning match.
    Hollar boys, hollar boys, ring bells ring,
    Hollar boys, hollar boys, God save the King!

A penny loaf to feed old Pope,
        a farthing cheese to choke him,
A pint of beer to rinse it down,
        a faggot of sticks to burn him.
Burn him in a tub of tar!
        burn him like a blazing star!
Burn his body from his head
        - then we'll say old Pope is dead.
Hip hip hoorah! Hip hip hoorah! Hip hip hoorah!

Bonfire 'Prayers' at Lewes

The survival of Bonfire Night in Lewes has been frequently attributed to the strength of nonconformity in the town, but the public display of excess in which the Bonfire Boys conducted themselves provoked steadfast condemnation if not active opposition from this quarter. The vast majority of Bonfire Boys and their wealthy supporters were Anglican and not members of the town's numerous nonconformist sects. Rather than being an expression of nonconformity, the Bonfire Boys' anti-Catholic stance is rooted in the 'Church and King' tradition of popular Protestantism in which the Church of England was seen as the national church and a bulwark against the political and religious aspirations of the Papacy.

Jim Etherington: 'Lewes Bonfire Night'

Membership of the town's various bonfire societies has always been a family affair involving mothers and daughters as well as fathers and sons, grandmothers as well as grandfathers and a whole collection of aunts, uncles and cousins. Many a Lewesian has his or her first bonfire experience as a babe in arms - perhaps as a papoose with Commercial Square's Red Indians or a fur clad bundle on a sled with Cliffe's Vikings. Each succeeding generation grows up with the bonfire tradition and with a loyalty to a particular society.

Brigid Chapman: 'Night of the Fires'

• Martyrs memorial,
Cliffe Hill, Lewes
198: TQ 424104

• Town Hall (formerly Star Inn), High Street, Lewes
198: TQ 415102

See 'Bloody Mary' in
<u>The Sussex Story</u>

ALONG KNOCKHUNDRED ROW

To the main road traveller, Midhurst, like Petworth, is a bewildering series of acute ninety-degree bends, combined with an inexplicable cottagey cosiness in the buildings, so different from the open market-places of Hampshire. Few towns are more deceptive, few towns withhold themselves so firmly until the traveller gets out of his car and on to his feet: few towns in particular have a more exciting relationship with the surrounding countryside.

Ian Nairn: 'The Buildings of England - Sussex'

Visitors can't be guaranteed a glimpse of George Aitchison's shock-headed young man, alas, but Midhurst retains the oddly unreconstructed air of a frontier in time and space: the gateway both to an earlier, slower-moving age, and to an area (those little-visited heathery commons) which stands apart.

H.G. Wells, whose mother was housekeeper at Uppark, (which becomes Bladesover in Tono-Bungay) worked briefly at a local chemist's shop, lodged over a tea shop and attended the Grammar School. The County Council has marked all three with plaques and has published an attractive booklet which explores the many literary references to West Sussex in the novels (much of The Invisible Man, for example, is set in Iping, to the north-west of Midhurst). Wells had a soft spot for the 'little old sunny rag-stone built town', which features as Wimblehurst in Tono-Bungay: 'I found something very agreeable in its clean, cobbled streets, its odd turnings and abrupt corners, and in the pleasant park that crowds up one side of the town.' In the park (see The Sussex Story*) are the ruins of the once-mighty Cowdray.*

West Sussex has a clutch of fine old market towns with ancient buildings lining their main streets, and I regret that no proper room can be found for three in particular: Horsham (OS map 187), especially around Carfax and along The Causeway to the church; East Grinstead (OS map 187), with its unusually wide High Street; and Steyning (OS map 198), with part-medieval houses at every turn.

Midhurst is a charming and peaceful little market-town with attractive old houses in one of the most beautiful regions of Sussex. It stands on the Western Rother about mid-way along the length of the delightful valley between Petersfield, just over the Hampshire border, and Pulborough, where the river joins the Arun. To the north extends a lovely range of the greensand hills, a little-visited country of open heathery commons and enchanting woods, while stretched out to the south is the escarpment of one of the best wooded sections of the South Downs.

F.R.Banks: 'The Penguin Guides - Sussex'

Although there are a number of handsome buildings in the main street, the finest group is to be found to the south-east up Knockhundred Row, in Church Hill and Red Lion Street. Here the collection of mainly sixteenth-, seventeenth- and eighteenth-century buildings forms the heart of the old town.

Michael H.C. Baker: 'Sussex Scenes'

It looks like a village in a fairy tale. There are high-gabled, black-timbered cottages here that seem the destined abode of witches. There is a butcher's shop where Red Riding Hood might enter to buy a rib of beef from the cow sold by Jack of Beanstalk fame. Outside the Spread Eagle, which does its best to live picturesquely up to its claim to be one of the oldest hostelries in England, there often sits a shock-headed youth in the costume that most of us attribute to Tom, the Piper's son. Midhurst indeed still manages to sit as the model for every old English village of the English pantomime.

George Aitchison: 'Sussex'

It is hard to separate Midhurst from Cowdray, the burnt out shell of which still stands in dignified dereliction down by the river. Once Queen Elizabeth I was lavishly entertained here, her household consuming three oxen and 140 geese for breakfast. Nowadays it is the polo rather than the provender that brings Prince Charles to Cowdray Park.

Brigid Chapman: 'Sussex - A Portrait in Colour'

- *Spread Eagle Hotel, Midhurst*
  197: SU 886215

- *Cowdray Ruins*
  (01730) 812215
  197: SU 891217

Midhurst buildings with H.G. Wells connections:

- *D. Morton Hickson's (chemist's shop, formerly S. E. Cowap) Church Street*
  197: SU 887215

- *Midhurst Grammar School, North Street*
  197: SU 886218

- *Ye Olde Tea Shoppe, North Street*
  197: SU 886216

- *Uppark, South Harting*
  (01730) 825415
  197: SU 779177

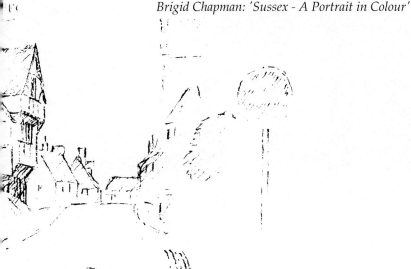

The Spread Eagle Hotel - Midhurst

Good nature writing appears effortless, but anyone who has tried it knows how readily the adjectives swarm, the senses swoon, the feelings gush. Tickner Edwardes mastered the art after forsaking his father's import-export business in London and moving to a remote cottage in Burpham. Here he wrote books and articles about country life (with an emphasis on the bee-keeping in which he specialised), as well as a number of fictional romances: *Tansy* was turned into a film, shot in Burpham itself in 1921.

Edwardes, who entered the priesthood in his fifties, became vicar of Burpham in 1927. John Cowper Powys, a neighbour, praised the man in typically strange terms. 'I always liked Mr Edwardes uncommonly well,' he wrote. 'I liked the tough-wood texture of his bodily presence!'

As these all too brief extracts reveal, Edwardes was a close observer of the natural world - like Thomas Hardy, he was 'a man who noticed such things'. The writing is richly descriptive without ever straining for the spiritual, for that deep personal fulfilment in leaf and flower which is the undoing of all but the finest practitioners.

There's humour, too. Imagine him on a downland summit such as Ditchling Beacon (illustrated here) in early May, the grass alive with butterflies which 'lingered fanning their wings luxuriously until some great bumble-bee arrived and pushed them off. For you can find the dreaded hustler everywhere in the world, even on a downland hill-top on a fine spring morning.'

MILK-WHITE DAWNS

Spring

There is only one scent on the countryside now. It pours in at the window on the first morning air. It meets you in every lane and meadow-path. Great aerial zones of its sweetness hover at the village street corners in the stillness of amber evening. Going out into the bee-garden under the star-gemmed summer dark, and stooping down to the threshold of any of the murmurous hives, you detect at once the same incense streaming hot and fragrant through the squad of fanning bees at every portal - the smell of hawthorn nectar brewing in tens of thousands of tiny vats within, to make the finest honey in the world.

— Ditchling Beacon from Westmeston —

Summer

You knew it was going to be a perfect summer's day from the beginning, by its gradual unfolding as of a perfect bud into the perfect flower. First, the night-mists tarried long into the dawn, and then drew away in softly voluted, sun-broidered sheets. And then the gentle breeze that had been stirring the cedar branches all the night neither quickened nor diminished with the rising sun, but held steadily on while the gold of the wood-top broadened and grew downwards until every leaf glade was aflare with the ever-kindling light. But surer token than any was the silence of the blackbirds: whereas the song thrushes were filling all the woods and wayside spinneys with a veritable tornado of music. Now, you get this chorus scarce ever without another certain sign of enduring summer weather, and instinctively you look away at once for it to the horizon. And there it is - a seam of milky violet joining earth and sky, with the distant hills already vaguely tremulous in its quivery depths.

Autumn

On these milk-white dawns of autumn the earliest sound of awakening life is so often a single bird singing: one lone bird in a tree-top darkly silhouetted against the morning sky. Today it was a thrush, and I stood in the dew-drenched undergrowth of the wood looking out through a trellis of dripping hazel-boughs at the old oak beyond, wherein I could clearly see him perched on one of the outermost branches, his breast swelling to the strain.

Winter

The great gorse patches on the Downs sing in the winter wind. In their shadows the grass is still grey with rime, but on their sunny sides the sward is drenched with the melted frost, big trembling gouts of water pendent from every blade, and giving back the level morning beams in a thousand points of rainbow light.

Tickner Edwardes: 'A Country Calendar'/'A Downland Year'

• Ditchling Beacon
198: TQ 331133

Where Tickner Edwardes lived:

• *Rycroft, Burpham (formerly Red Cottage, private)*
197: TQ 040089

• *Ilex Cottage, Burpham (private)*
197: TQ 044090

Where Tickner Edwardes is buried:

• *Burpham churchyard*
197: TQ 039090

Here we pay tribute to an ancient craft that has managed to survive into the modern age. Most of the blacksmith's former customers have gone, many a forge converted into a village garage (until that, too, has bowed to economic pressures), but leisure riding has provided a lasting demand for the farrier's arts.

Gaius Carley, who was born at Starnash Farm, Upper Dicker, in 1888, and worked in smithies across the county (at Blackboys, Framfield, Offham, Rotherfield, Horsham, Kirdford, Petworth, Northchapel, Pulborough and Adversane), published his colourful memoirs in 1963, with tales of hop-picking, bird-scaring and writing love letters for an illiterate gipsy alongside an evocation of life among the anvils and bellows. His boisterous Song of the Blacksmith, its metre hardly suggestive of the hammer's steady rhythm, first appeared in the West Sussex Gazette in 1959.

All crafts and trades once had their proud traditions, and blacksmiths celebrated the feast of their patron saint, St Clement, on November 23 - Old Clem Night. A literal highlight of the occasion was 'firing the anvil', which involved filling the hole beneath the anvil with gunpowder, plugging it and (from a safe distance) setting it alight. Frank Dean, who in his book recalls a firing that went not entirely according to plan, not only works in the forge where his father was a blacksmith before him, but has high hopes that his grandson will be the fourth generation to heat the coals at Rodmell.

JOLLY WELL TOUGH

Nearly sixty years work in the jolly old forge,
Sometimes pleasant, sometimes rough,
Trying to please horses and horsemen,
It's made me jolly well tough.

Some horses were wicked and spiteful,
And made my legs wobble and bend,
Then in the Blacksmiths Arms I'd go
For a pint and an hour to spend.

The old forge is getting more draughty,
And the iron tyre bender has fallen down,
For when the wheels want rerubbering
They are taken to the nearest town.

The anvil is getting uneven
My bellows begin to wheeze,
And the hammers seem to get heavier,
The vice and the drills harder to squeeze.

The tyreing platform is useless,
It was fixed near the old roasting jacks,
And nearly all old village blacksmiths
Are laid out stiff on their backs.

Some clients were bad-mannered and ungrateful,
Very often I swore and despaired,
After I had eased their corns and bruises
And their stinking feet manicured.

I will beat out the white hot metal
Till all that is left of me is skin and bone,
And when I hear the last tingle of the anvil
I will know it's time to go home.

When I go up the pearly paved pathway,
The doorkeeper will shout 'Don't you know
That the place for most village blacksmiths
Is stoked to white heat down below?'

I will tell him he's mistaken or ignorant,
'There is no two places like that I'm sure.
I've left it, so beg my pardon,
And very soon open the door.'

For I bow only to the great forger of all things
Who knows for man and beast I've striven,
He will say 'Come in at once,
Your sweary sins are all forgiven.'

Gaius Carley: 'The Song of the Blacksmith'

One of my father's favourite sayings was, 'Never stand behind a horse or in front of a judge.'

We have had very difficult horses at times, plenty of them, but we don't get kicked very often. Mostly we get trodden on, but quite often it's torn hands. This happens when we are holding the feet with the nails through and the horse moves. I've got scars all over my hands caused by this.

I've also got a tidy old scar on my leg from a very quiet cart horse. He straightened his leg out and put it to the ground and as he did so the nail went in and tore my leg open. I was here shoeing on my own that day (mother and father had gone to London), so I couldn't leave to go to the doctor. I had to wrap a big towel around my leg as it was bleeding so much, and finish shoeing the horse.

Oxen shoeing was a bit before my time. I believe the last oxen teams to be used on farms hereabouts were by Percy Gorringe at Exceat in 1925 and Major Harding at Birling Manor Farm in late 1928 or early 1929. However, I once shod a bull to help straighten his legs. This was known as remedial shoeing. He was a quiet enough animal, and I had trimmed his feet up several times before. He belonged to Norman Stacey at Southease and was later sold as a stock bull.

The shire stallions travelled the countryside visiting the farms to cover the mares. We shod the last travelling stallion in the 1930s, one from Essex named Copthall Tarzan. He travelled this area for several years, coming down in March till about July and was based at Stanmer Park. On a Monday he went through to Lewes Market, then stopped off here to be shod. Then on down to Dean's Farm at Piddinghoe where he stopped overnight. The next day he travelled on to Bishopstone and visited other farms on the way to Jevington for another overnight stop. From there he meandered up through to the Roebuck at Laughton. Next day on to the Five Bells at Chailey and on Friday back to Stanmer for the weekend - a very busy lad!

Frank Dean: 'Strike While the Iron's Hot'

• Frank Dean's forge, Rodmell (above) 198: TQ 418059

Other working forges at:

• Weald &Downland Open Air Museum, Singleton (01243) 811348 197: SU 875128

• Amberley Chalkpits Museum (01798) 831831 197: TQ 031123

Chanctonbury Ring may, properly speaking, be the earthwork that circles this 779ft (238m) hilltop - Iron Age settlers, the Romans and the Saxons were all here - but in the popular understanding it is the grove of beech trees planted in 1760 by the nineteen-year-old heir to the Wiston Estate, Charles Goring: 'the crown and symbol of the South Downs,' as Miles Jebb puts it in his guide to the South Downs Way.

Some other downland summits are higher, but this clump of trees has given Chanctonbury a special place in Sussex affections, visible as it is for many miles around. 'Walkers on the Surrey hills pause to look for it in the blue distance. Sailors mark it from their ships in the Channel. Its likeness has gone round the world by picture postcard and illustrated book,' wrote Ben Darby, adding ominously: 'But a practical forester would never have planted anything up there on the hilltop. Chanctonbury stands slap in the path of the south-west gales that rage in from the Channel with nothing to break their force.'

Those lines were written before the great storm of October 1987, which felled many of the beeches and left others in sorry tatters - an ill wind that blew kindly, at least, on the archaeologists who were suddenly given new opportunities to excavate the site. Charles Goring, we can be sure, would have wept. Yet the ring of trees remains, defiant if rather less than glorious, and those of us who love it must ever be willing its regeneration, by natural means or otherwise.

— Chanctonbury Ring —

OLD MOTHER GORING

'Old Mother Goring's got her cap on; we shall soon have wet.'

Sussex weather lore

From Chanctonbury Ring nearly all Sussex can be seen. It is a wonderful panorama and few in the south of England rival it.

Arthur Mee: 'The King's England - Sussex'

I veered right-handed keeping on the broad upper shoulders of the crest, and saw before me the huge clump of Chanctonbury beeches ahead, moulded by the wind into the likeness of a great porcupine's back.

S.P.B Mais: 'Hills of the South'

> *How oft around thy Ring, sweet Hill,*
> *A boy, I used to play,*
> *And form my plans to plant thy top*
> *On some auspicious day.*
> *How oft among thy broken turf*
> *With what delight I trod,*
> *With what delight I placed those twigs*
> *Beneath thy maiden sod.*
> *And then an almost hopeless wish*
> *Would creep within my breast,*
> *Oh! could I live to see thy top*
> *In all its beauty dress'd.*
> *That time's arrived; I've had my wish,*
> *And lived to eighty-five;*
> *I'll thank my God who gave such grace*
> *As long as e'er I live.*
> *Still when the morning sun in Spring,*
> *Whilst I enjoy my sight,*
> *Shall gild thy new-clothed beech and sides,*
> *I'll view thee with delight.*

Charles Goring

It was that blue view of Chanctonbury which gave me in childhood my first conscious feeling of the beauty of the visible world and the mystery of the invisible. Standing in the rough matted grass of a neglected field, looking westward, with the great line of the Downs sweeping towards a sunset sky where the headland of Chanctonbury floated like something of another world, beauty took hold of me, consciously and inescapably - the curious ache of it, and the troubling for the first time laid on the young resilient heart.

Years later an old Sussex countrywoman, looking on nearly the same scene with time-worn eyes, said to me: 'It does something to you.'

It does.

Esther Meynell: 'Sussex'

- *Chanctonbury Ring*
  198: TQ 139121

Some other downland summits, east to west (with height in feet/metres):

- *Beachy Head (534/163)*
  199: TV 583951

- *Willingdon Hill (636/194)*
  199: TQ 579024

- *Firle Beacon (712/217)*
  198: TQ 486059

- *Newmarket Hill (646/197)*
  198: TQ 364070

- *Blackcap (676/206)*
  198: TQ 374126

- *Ditchling Beacon (813/248)*
  198: TQ 331133
  (see illustration, p. 51)

- *Newtimber Hill (663/202)*
  198: TQ 274125

- *Devil's Dyke (712/217)*
  198: TQ 258109

- *Truleigh Hill (709/216)*
  198: 225108

- *Kithurst Hill (699/213)*
  197: TQ 082125

- *Rackham Hill (633/193)*
  197: TQ 053126

- *Bignor Hill (738/225)*
  197: SU 983136

- *Burton Down (804/245)*
  197: SU 966132

- *Littleton Down (837/255)*
  197: SU 942150

- *Treyford Hill (771/235)*
  197: SU 830177

- *Beacon Hill (794/242)*
  197: SU 807184

FRENCH AND FEUDAL

To visit the parish church at Arundel is to discover the drama of the town's feudal and ecclesiastical history given permanent physical expression. The chancel is blocked off by a glass screen, through which you see an array of imposing tombs. The odd fact is that the nave of the church is Anglican while the chancel (the Fitzalan Chapel) is Roman Catholic. It can be visited, but only by way of the grounds of Arundel Castle.

The story of this strange arrangement begins in 1380, when a college of secular priests was granted exclusive use of the chancel. At the dissolution of the monasteries, Henry VIII sold it to the Earl of Arundel, Henry Fitzalan - whose daughter and heiress, Mary, was later to marry the fourth Duke of Norfolk. Cromwell's troops badly damaged the church during a Civil War bombardment of the castle, and when the nave was repaired the east end was blocked off. A bold Victorian vicar took on the great lord and demanded his chancel back, but a High Court ruling of 1880 established that it was, indeed, the property of the Premier Duke. The Roman Catholics of the town worshipped here until the 15th Duke built them their own church - now the Cathedral of Our Lady and St Philip Howard.

If the extract from Titus Groan appears whimsical, the fact is that Mervyn Peake began writing his strange trilogy while he was living in a cottage near Burpham (94 Wepham), the walls and turrets of Arundel Castle rearing up beyond the river to be transformed into the fantastic Gormenghast of his imagination.

Castle, cathedral, church - these are Arundel; the town itself is secondary, subordinate, feudal. The castle is what one likes a castle to be - a mass of battlemented stone, with a keep, a gateway and a history.

E.V. Lucas: 'Highways and Byways in Sussex'

Arundel is everyone's idea of what an ancient town should be: a steep street of old buildings rising from a peaceful river, a huge church on the crest of the hill, the soaring towers of a castle against a backcloth of park and woodland.

Keith Spence: 'The Companion Guide to Kent and Sussex'

A first astonished glance from the train will make you think that you are in France. There, in profile, a great Gothic castle and cathedral crouch over a beautiful little town standing in a flat, marshy plain. From a distance they look superb, and have been called with justice one of the great town views in England.

Desmond Seward: 'Sussex'

The town does not look quite English even when you get into it. One long street climbs the hill, little streets lead off it, and houses of various age, size and shape stand

cheek by jowl, usually flush with the road. It is an attractive architectural medley.

Ben Darby: 'View of Sussex'

This is a vision which the quiet mind does not easily forget, the vision of Arundel from Crossbush Hill in the haze of an early summer morning, with all the world abed, with the dew on the grass and the lark overhead, and the sunshine dancing on the roofs and spires and turrets of a faery town suspended from the sky on threads of gossamer.

Francis D. Allison: 'The Little Town of Arundel'

Gormenghast, that is, the main massing of the original stone, taken by itself would have displayed a certain ponderous architectural quality were it possible to have ignored the circumfusion of those mean dwellings that swarmed like an epidemic around its outer walls. They sprawled over the sloping earth, each one half way over its neighbour until, held back by the castle ramparts, the innermost of these hovels laid hold on the great walls, clamping themselves thereto like limpets to a rock. These dwellings, by ancient law, were granted this chill intimacy with the stronghold that loomed above them. Over their irregular roofs would fall throughout the seasons, the shadows of time-eaten buttresses, of broken and lofty turrets.

Mervyn Peake: 'Titus Groan'

— *Arundel from the road to Warningcamp* —

- *Arundel Church*
197: TQ 015073

- *Arundel Castle*
(01903) 883136
197: TQ 018073

- *Arundel Cathedral*
(01903) 882297
197: TQ 015072

Nearby attraction:

- *Wildfowl & Wetlands Trust, Mill Road, Arundel*
(01903) 883355
197: TQ 022080

Tourist Information
(01903) 882268

Where Mervyn Peake is buried:

- *Burpham churchyard*
197: TQ 039090

Some other Sussex castles (and see The Sussex Story*):*

- *Bramber*
(English Heritage)
198: TQ 184107

- *Lewes*
(Sussex Archaeological Society)
(01273) 474379
198: TQ 414101

- *Pevensey*
(English Heritage)
(01323) 762604
199: TQ 644048

- *Hastings*
(01424) 717963
199: TV 822094

- *Bodiam*
(National Trust)
(01580) 830436
188: TQ 785256

AN ANCIENT ROAD

While the chief north-south roads of Sussex rush pell-mell towards the coast, most of the east-west routes are happily content to amble. Hilaire Belloc's walk across the county in 'The Four Men' began at The George in Robertsbridge and ended at South Harting, so that it was only during the latter part of his journey (from Steyning westwards) that he followed the course he describes here, hard under the northern scarp of the Downs. It is, as it happens, my own favourite road, or series of roads, and (oh, lucky man!) my home fits snugly within a bend of it under Ditchling Beacon.

Belloc's litany of names requires a little glossing. The 'vale of Glynde' is Glynleigh Level on the Pevensey Marshes; Coombe Place at Offham points us to 'the edge of the Combe'; Courthouse Farm, with its cluster of flint buildings, is below Blackcap and Mount Harry on B2116; 'Clinton' is Clayton; and 'Hollow Pie Combe' is Pyecombe.

To explore this ancient route and its byways is to discover inviting towns and villages (Alfriston, Lewes, Steyning, Amberley); a wide variety of 'attractions' (the Clergy House at Alfriston, Parham House near Storrington, Bignor Roman Villa) and a host of such homely downland churches as the candlelit St Andrew's at Didling in that sleepy, relatively unknown, area close to the Hampshire border.

By the Shepherd & Dog pub at Fulking the pure water does, indeed, gush out as Belloc describes it. 'He sendeth springs into the valleys,' reads a Victorian plaque, 'which run among the hills.'

So all along the road under Chanctonbury, that high hill, we went as the morning broadened, along a way that is much older than anything in the world: a way that leads from old Pevensey Port through the vale of Glynde and across Cuckmere and across Ouse and then up to the height of Lewes, and then round the edge of the Combe, and then down on to the ledge below the Downs, making Court House and Plumpton Corner, West Meston, Clinton, and

Hollow Pie Combe (though between these two it branches and meets again, making an island of Wolstonbury Hill), and then on by Poynings and Fulking and Edburton, and so to the crossing of the water and the Fort of Bramber, and so along and along all under the Downs until it passes Arun at Houghton Bridge, and so by Bury and Westburton, and Sutton and Duncton, Graffham and Cocking, Didling and Harting - all Sussex names and all places where the pure water, having dripped through the chalk of the high hills, gushes out in fountains to feed that line of steadings and of human homes.

Hilaire Belloc: 'The Four Men'

The Castle - Lewes

Clayton

Ditchling

Robertsbridge

Lewes

Alfriston

Pevensey

It shouldn't have worked at all - but it worked twice over.

In 1933 John Christie announced to a puzzled world that the opera house he was building in the grounds of his Tudor country house would open the following season. A case of potty self-indulgence? Opera houses, after all, were always found in cities, and this one would be a stage for Christie's soprano wife, Audrey Mildmay. Yet Glyndebourne (picnic hampers and all) rapidly earned an international reputation - and for the quality of its productions as much as for the uniqueness of its garden setting.

The second part of the story is equally remarkable. In 1994, displaying the same flair and acumen as his father, Sir George Christie built a completely new, and considerably larger, opera house on the site, financed without a penny of public money. He had, he later confessed, three major worries: that it wouldn't be finished in time; that he might not be able to raise the cash; and that the theatre would prove to be, as he put it, 'duff'. In fact the new Glyndebourne, which opened sixty years to the day after the first one and with the very same opera (Mozart's The Marriage of Figaro), was an instant success, winning awards for its architects - Michael and Patty Hopkins - and close to unanimous acclaim from performers and audiences alike.

New, but recognisable to those who loved the old place: 'While the sheep are there,' Robert Tear told Opera Now magazine, 'it will never be just another opera house.'

OPERA WITH PICNICS

Perhaps if in 1933 we had known about the absence of a stage door at Glyndebourne we might have had some clue to the nature of the whole project; or, if not, at any rate have been instinctively more suspicious of it. No stage door would mean no stage door keeper; and no stage door keeper would mean there were no autograph hunters to keep away, and - even more significant - none of those numberless, nameless, whispering conspiratorial figures with briefcases who haunt the doorways, anterooms and staircases of the rest of the world's opera houses. Here, we would have known at once, was uniqueness indeed.

Spike Hughes: 'Glyndebourne'

We have aimed to build a theatre without pretensions - there is no plush velvet and gilt - and to go for simplicity with style, of form and of craftmanship.

Sir George Christie , opening the new Glyndebourne, May 1994

The little 'thirties opera house blended with the landscape - since John Christie built with weathered brick and tiles - and I do not like the vast new opera house which has replaced it, a horseshoe of red brick and metal plating, but the auditorium is magnificent. I am grateful for the ugly monster as it means that at last I shall be able to obtain tickets - whose rarity was a source of much local grumbling.

Desmond Seward: 'Sussex'

Communication with the audience is unspeakably wonderful simply because you can see them all, so you know you don't have to strain for their attention. In the old house you couldn't see to the back, whereas this one is all around you and encircling.

Robert Tear, Don Basilio on the opening night of the new theatre

Architecturally I think it's absolutely brilliant. Acoustically it's very clear, very crisp and slightly clinical.

Nicholas Kenyon, Controller, BBC Radio 3

We can hear one another play. In the old place we were always being told to play down because we were drowning the singers. We now seem to be able to let rip happily and play pretty well as we would in a concert hall. We've had lots of people leaning over and saying how wonderful it sounds.

Richard Bissill, Principal Horn, London Philharmonic

One of the great joys of Glyndebourne is gazing at everyone else and there is a whole area for doing that on each floor and also throughout the bar area.

Joan Bakewell

No other opera house has a garden for its foyer.

Mary Christie: 'Glyndebourne, the Gardens'

The gardens of Glyndebourne have many different meanings for those who visit them. To the convivial they offer a perfect picnic spot where they can nibble smoked salmon and pop a cork or two. To the urban, they are a paradise where they can stroll in innocent wonder gazing at the charming landscape and the apparently spontaneous bursts of flowers. To the gardening connoisseur they are a field of study which they tour with their fellow initiates admiring, criticising, identifying with no more than a sideways glance at the labels. To me, they represent tranquillity. Inside the opera house Anna Bolena may be singing her head off as she kneels at the block, Don Giovanni may be descending into hell, or Macbeth staring transfixed at the Apparition of the Bloody Child, but outside, the gardens smile with the serenity which only a tradition of centuries can bring.

Anne Scott-James: 'Glyndebourne, the Gardens'

The Bourne garden is the surprise package. With show-off staircases cribbed from Covent Garden, and plants that are more Stravinsky than Rossini, it has a different spirit from the rest. Might this perhaps appeal more to the new Glyndebourne customers in the seats at the top of the house, than to the old guard? The steps, which will one day be covered in camomile and thyme, are large enough to picnic on, and the views from the top path are matchless.

Mary Keen: 'Glyndebourne, the Gardens'

• Glyndebourne
Opera House
(01273) 812321 (admin)
(01273) 813813 (box office)
198: TQ 453108

Nearby attraction:

• Glynde Place
(01273) 858337
198: TQ 456093

Other Sussex festival venues:

• Chichester Festival
Theatre, Oaklands Park,
Chichester
(01243) 784437
197: SU 863054

• Theatre Royal,
New Road, Brighton
(01273) 327480
198: TQ 312042

• The Hawth,
Hawth Avenue, Crawley
(01293) 553636
187: TQ 278362

— Glyndebourne —

POOH'S ENCHANTED PLACE

The great ironmasters coppiced large areas of Ashdown Forest to fuel their greedy furnaces, but it's the obstinate, sometimes violent, Commoners that we have to thank for our enjoyment of these breezy tracts of heath and scrub today - walking or riding on the Forest, in local parlance, rather than in it. They successfully resisted the attempts of powerful landowners to enclose the area (and so take away their rights to graze animals on the waste, cut bracken for bedding and fell birches for firewood, fencing and the building of their hovels) until, in 1693 (see The Sussex Story), the law came down on the side of the underdog. Nowadays the clearance of invasive bracken, birch and Scots pine - vital work if the distinctive heathland flora and fauna are to survive - falls to the Conservators and their volunteer army.

For all that the place has a turbulent past, its presiding genius is a gentle little bear with a great fondness for honey. A.A. Milne lived at Cotchford Farm on the edge of Hartfield, and he put the Forest in his books with little disguise. (The bridge where the friends played Poohsticks is the devil to find, but has been restored by East Sussex County Council). In the case of his son, Christopher Robin - mercilessly teased at school, endlessly pursued by Pooh fans for the rest of his life - the verisimilitude was too exact for comfort.

E.H. Shepard, whose drawings are inseparable from Milne's text, shares a monument with him at Gills Lap - a typical Forest high spot with wonderful extensive views.

By and by they came to an enchanted place on the very top of the Forest called Galleons Lap, which is sixty-something trees in a circle; and Christopher Robin knew that it was enchanted because nobody had ever been able to count whether it was sixty-three or sixty-four, not even when he tied a piece of string round each tree after he had counted it. Being enchanted, its floor was not like the floor of the Forest, gorse and bracken and heather, but close-set grass, quiet and smooth and green. Sitting there they could see the whole world spread out until it reached the sky.

A.A. Milne: 'The House at Pooh Corner'

I could see Gills Lap from my nursery window - a clump of pines on the top of a hill. And of course you can see it as Shepard drew it in 'The House at Pooh Corner'. In the book it is Galleons Lap but otherwise it is exactly as described, an enchanted spot before ever Pooh came along to add to its magic.

Christopher Milne: 'The Enchanted Places'

In late summer, colonies of bog asphodel infuse the sphagnum bogs with a golden glow and wisps of white cotton grass bend before the winds. The rare marsh gentians flourish on a few stretches of damp heath, though their numbers tend to fluctuate for reasons not yet explained. On warm summer nights when moths are abundant, the weird churring and wing-clapping of nightjars may be heard amid the bracken and gorse. Occasionally, the odd pair of hobbies nesting in some scattered clump of Scots pines may be seen pouncing upon the grasshoppers and dragonflies; and the evocative calls of nesting curlew are sometimes heard amid the bleached purple moor grass and heather.

Garth Christian: 'Ashdown Forest'

Autumn cannot fail to offer more than any other time. Spring is just spring, exuberant, delicate and a bit silly, following the inevitable pattern, an infinity of subtly differing greens, bluebell, wood anemone - few primroses here. When the bracken first breaks through it has some charm, acres of mock asparagus far removed from that later sea, so heavy and unvaried, so downright boring. The initial hint of better things comes after the orchids, the first-footer among the heathers, delicately pink and immensely welcome. There is a fractional pause, then, almost a change of light. The purple heathers take up the theme, with *erica tetralix*, the close-leaved heath, surely the winner for its exuberant colour and dark sharp leaf. The less well coloured ling then takes over, swamping all. Sheets of the stuff are spread like tented cloth. As if infected by the basic dye, the bracken begins to turn. When this happens it is difficult to understand why one has ever supposed it a mere invader. It complements all, not least the marsh gentian which is the Forest's pride. Impossible, when bracken is at the peak of its colour, to have too much of it - or so many of us claim. It is not only autumn, either, that gives it so long a splendour - wet winter restores colour to the battered rows and they glow again.

Barbara Willard: 'The Forest - Ashdown in East Sussex'

Ashdown Forest

It is a tract of singular loveliness, one of the few surviving vestiges of primeval England.

Peter Brandon: 'The Sussex Landscape'

No matter how often you go there, it always seems new, and always a place apart. The Forest does not claim you, and you do not claim the Forest. You are always a visitor. But it fascinates. It is irresistible.

Ben Darby: 'Journey Through the Weald'

So off they went together. But wherever they go, and whatever happens to them on the way, in that enchanted place on the top of the Forest a little boy and his bear will always be playing.

A.A. Milne: 'The House at Pooh Corner'

It seemed to me, almost, that my father had got to where he was by climbing upon my infant shoulders, that he had filched from me my good name and had left me with nothing but the empty fame of being his son.

Christopher Milne: 'The Enchanted Places'

• *Ashdown Forest*
OS maps 187, 188, 189

•*Visitor centre, Wych Cross*
(01342) 823583
187: TQ 433324

• *Milne/Shepard memorial,*
Gills Lap
188: TQ 468320

• *Poohsticks Bridge*
188: TQ 470338

Where E.H. Shepard is buried:
• *Lodsworth churchyard*
197: SU 931228

See <u>Living Sussex</u> *for the wildlife of the Forest*

THE UNWRITTEN MULTITUDES

Yet Sussex, simple-hearted, loves not her great ones best,
But minds the unwritten multitudes she bore upon her breast,
The woodman, craftsman, husbandman, who wrought and hewed and tilled,
All quiet souls who day by day their day's work well fulfilled.

F.W. Bourdillon: 'In Praise of Sussex'

The average Downland peasant is large-limbed and loose of build. His gait is either slow and shambling or heavy and deliberate. Grace is the last thing to be associated with his movements. You might think that he suffered from chronic fatigue, but in reality his lumbering walk is due mainly to a want of physical training and the matter of his occupation, which favours slow movements.

Arthur Beckett: 'The Spirit of the Downs'

It is a fact, I think, that there is a streak or vein of stupidity, which, running eastward from Hampshire, crops up in many places among the West Sussex Downs. One day, seeing a youth harnessing a pony at a gate, I asked him the name of a hill over which I had just walked. 'I don't know,' he returned, evidently surprised at the question; 'I never heard that it had a name.' A hill, I assured him, must have a name; and I remarked that he was probably new to the neighbourhood. He assured me that he was a native of the place, and that to his knowledge the hill had no name; then he added casually, 'We call it Bepton Hill.'

W.H. Hudson: 'Nature in Downland'

A man's ability was reckoned by the strength of his muscles and if a lad could lift a hundredweight he got a job and no other qualifications were considered necessary. Strong men were admired and tales of their achievements lived on. Old Alfie Teale was a man of remarkable strength and stood almost as wide as he was high. 'He was a short-arsed little bugger - 'e'd 'ave to climb up a ladder to look down a well.' But with his exceedingly long arms - 'E could button up 'is leggin's without bendin' 'is back' - he could carry a two and a quarter hundredweight sack of barley under each arm.

Bob Copper: 'A Song for Every Season'

Call him Hobsman - he has had many names - he is the one essential human figure when all the shows and shadows of glory are gone. He is seen under sun and rain, immense and processional - processional through the seasons and the centuries, through generations of human lives, engaged in the same unending, elementary and requiting toil. The tilling and sowing of the earth is the first step man makes from pastoral savagery.

Esther Meynell: 'A Woman Talking'

A strong family likeness wavered in and out of the fierce, earth-reddened faces of the seven, like a capricious light. Micah Starkadder, mightiest of the cousins, was a ruined giant of a man, paralysed in one knee and wrist. His nephew, Urk, was a little, red,

---

The nobility of sweated toil is perhaps more easily recognised by the spectator than by the poor wretch with the damp brow and aching limbs who ought to have (and does here) the last word on the subject, but we shouldn't dismiss out of hand the tribute of Edward Thomas, a writer best known for his first world war poems, but who wrote several books about the English countryside and devotes a good part of The South Country to Sussex. Life on our farms has changed utterly within a few generations, and an onlooker may at least ask whether the solitary tractor driver, isolated and insulated in his cab with only a pair of headphones for company, has lost some vital component of the job along with the worst of the drudgery.

*A contemplation of the Rev. Bourdillon's 'quiet souls' (what an excellent title he found for his poem) seems a useful test of a writer's humanity. Esther Meynell, whose books are well worth searching out, displays a reverence akin to Bourdillon's and Thomas's;**Bob Copper (see p. 12)**mixes humour and respect; while Arthur Beckett looks down from a lofty height upon creatures only a little removed from the beasts of the field. This would seem a pretty good description of the Starkadders in Cold Comfort Farm, a novel set in deepest rural Sussex, but Stella Gibbons's comic classic - 'Big Business bellowed again. It was a harsh, mournful sound; there were old swamps and rotting horns buried in it' - is a satire on melodramatic romances rather than on farming folk themselves.*

hard-bitten man with foxy ears. Urk's brother, Ezra, was of the same physical type, but horsy where Urk was foxy. Caraway, a silent man, wind-shaven and lean, with long wandering fingers, had some of Seth's animal grace, and this had been passed on to his son, Harkaway, a young, silent, nervous man given to bursts of fury about very little, when you came to sift matters.

Amos, who was even larger and more of a wreck than Micah, silently put his pruning-snoot and reaping-hook in a corner by the fender, while Reuben put the scranlet with which he had been ploughing down beside them.

Stella Gibbons: 'Cold Comfort Farm'

Eastwick Barn, which lies beyond Standean, due east of Patcham, was the last place round here where I saw threshing done by hand with a flail. As you stand and watch a powerful man regularly swinging his flail it looks quite a simple operation; but try it, and you will find it is quite easy to get a nasty rap on the head.

Frederick F. Wood: 'Round About Sussex Downs'

Tuesday August 24. All hands on dung cart to fallow in Carters field. I see to the sheep and help Banfield set up blown down shocks in Uptons. In the afternoon Hunt starts cutting in Rushetts but has to leave off after two rounds owing to rain. Banfield and I cut out dodder patches in clover in Crab Tree. Moore and Steve go hurdle cart from the Gurze to tares and rape in Old Woods. Weather: another wet miserable afternoon and evening.

William Carter Swan: 'The Diary of a Farm Apprentice'

Stately walks the carter's boy with his perpendicular brass-bound whip, alongside four wagon-horses, while the carter rides. It is a pleasant thing to see them going to their work in the early gold of the morning, fresh, silent, their horses jingling, down the firm road. If they were leading their team to yoke them to the chariot of the sun they could not be more noble.

Edward Thomas: 'The South Country'

I used to take them out ploughing or log-hauling and even carting out dung. It was on a place about two miles from our house so I had a two-mile walk before I even started work. I was in the stables before seven o'clock in the morning and didn't finish till five and then I had to walk all the way home. It was all right in the summer but it was a bugger in the winter with the wind and rain coming in from the coast and great big potholes, what they called 'stopples', in the road, that you sank in up to your knees if you was little.

Gilbert Sargent: 'A Sussex Life'

I can't say that I always enjoyed work. Going back to my early days on the farm, as a young boy of eleven and a half years old, I sometimes hated it, especially on the hills in winter time. With two horses and a plough we were expected to cover an acre a day - today with a tractor a man can plough six acres an hour! I've lived through two world wars, and all the time we were urged to plough up more ground to grow more food. Today farmers are paid *not* to grow food, but to set their land 'aside'. They say there's a surplus, yet there are millions of starving people in the world. To me it doesn't make sense.

Harold Cannings: 'Follow the Plough'

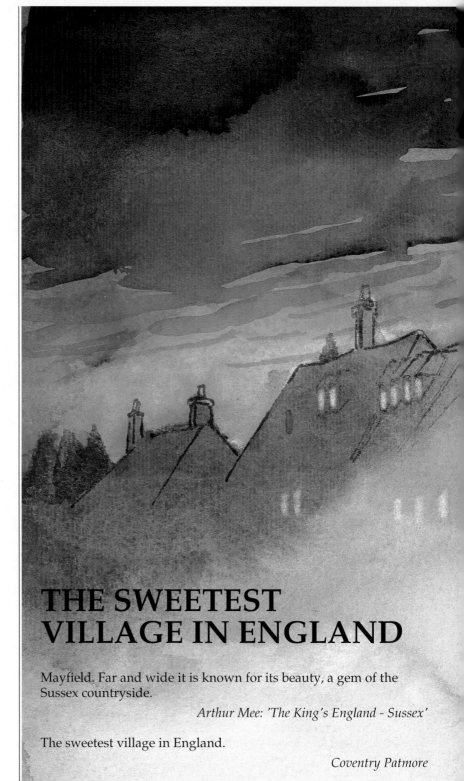

Mayfield is one of several villages built on the ridges and hilltops of the High Weald (Burwash is another), and I have spent several happy hours of my life sitting in the garden of the rambling sixteenth century Middle House inn, gazing south over the Rother Valley to the Heathfield region and far beyond. It's a lovely village. On the other side of a High Street lined with ancient buildings is the large parish church, several of its headstones graced by the pretty terracotta plaques - cherubs, vases, baskets of fruit - which were the speciality of the Heathfield stonemason Jonathan Harmer (1762-1849) and which can be found in many churchyards in this part of the county.

The High Weald, running south-east from Ashdown Forest to meet the sea at the fossil-rich cliffs of Hastings, was the centre of the great iron industry which provided the Tudors with their armaments: the church contains iron grave slabs; Middle House was built for an ironmaster; and a cannon dug out of one of the cinder beds of the Mayfield furnace is on display in the High Street.

St Leonards-Mayfield School at the top of the hill incorporates the remains of a palace of the Archbishops of Canterbury, Pevsner declaring its chapel to be 'one of the most spectacular medieval halls of England'. A local man, St Dunstan, was himself Archbishop of Canterbury from 960 to 988: on the colourful village sign he tussles with his legendary adversary, the Devil, who tried to tempt him in the guise of a young girl but was betrayed by a tell-tale cloven hoof.

THE SWEETEST VILLAGE IN ENGLAND

Mayfield. Far and wide it is known for its beauty, a gem of the Sussex countryside.

Arthur Mee: 'The King's England - Sussex'

The sweetest village in England.

Coventry Patmore

The best way to approach it is from the south. Then you see it almost as a southern European hill village, flowing down from the church on the topmost point. It is a splendid picture when the morning sun plays upon the flank of the hill.

Ben Darby: 'Journey Through the Weald'

One locality retaining much of its earlier aspect of a medieval clearing lies south-west of Mayfield, a beautiful hilltop village of medieval and sixteenth century half-timbered houses overlooking the remote watershed of the rivers Ouse and Rother. In this deeply secluded pocket of the High Weald, where a tangle of narrow lanes and bridleways still preserves its air of quietness and mystery, are the scattered farms called Reed (a name derived from the Middle English *ridde*, meaning to grub trees) - Great and Little Broad Reed, Stile Reed and Wood Reed Farms. These were created by pioneers who took up successive grants of assart land from the reeve of the Archbishop of Canterbury's manor of South Malling and carved steep fields out of the wild during the thirteenth century.

Seventeenth century developments helped to compose the present mine pits in the woods, hop-growing (so creating the need for the picturesque oast houses) and the farmhouse rebuilding which added tile-hung and weather-boarded fronts. Nevertheless, the rural ground plan with its thickly timbered shaws, wayside hazel coppice, greenways bordered by marl pits, and small fields sloping away to the humble, unregarded farmhouses almost lost to sight amid trees in the hollows is, in essence, the work of the Age of Clearance. That such unspoiled traditional countryside should survive within forty-five miles of central London is one of many unexpected delights of the Sussex High Weald.

Peter Brandon: 'The Sussex Landscape'

• *Mayfield Church*
188/199: TQ 586270

• *St Leonards-Mayfield School*
(The Old Palace; private, but visits can be arranged)
(01435) 873055
188/199: TQ 587271

• *Broadreed Farm*
188/199: TQ 548253

The artist J.M.W.Turner discovered his mature style at Petworth, where he was the guest of the art-loving third Earl of Egremont. In this treasure-store, however, Turner's pictures have to share the glory with works by, among others, Van Dyck, William Blake and ('the most superb monument to his skill,' Horace Walpole thought) the woodcarver Grinling Gibbons.

The west front of the house has been described as the closest approximation in England to a chateau in the grand manner of Louis XIV's France, and there's an austerity about the state rooms inside, but the park with its large herd of fallow deer is unquestionably English: landscaped by the young Capability Brown to create a broad vista of pastureland, lake and trees against a backdrop of the Downs. Entrance to the park is free.

No Sussex town suffers more from traffic congestion than Petworth (our picture shows the grand house behind the unusual lamp standard designed by Charles Barry, architect of the Houses of Parliament) but the narrow, twisting streets running from the compact Market Square should be explored on foot - as Walter Wilkinson would vehemently assert were he still with us. A Sussex Peepshow is the tale of a spring and summer spent pushing his Punch and Judy on a barrow through Sussex, earning pennies whenever he could discover an audience to enjoy a performance. An educated and humorous man, Wilkinson produced a one-off book which demands the use of that overworked encomium, delightful.

URBANITY WITHOUT POVERTY

Few English towns can catch the heart now from outside: too much has been added around them too recently and without enough love. But Petworth still can, though it can only be seen at a distance, from the South Downs or its foothills. Petworth is on the sandstone ridge which answers the Downs about four miles to the north, and the slope is shallow enough to show the town as though it were on a tilted plate. Around it green fields on both sides, the big house on the left, the rose-red church tower in the middle - an image of urbanity without poverty.

Ian Nairn: 'The Buildings of England: Sussex'

The very police station at Petworth, a grim enough place discreetly hid, has so glorious a view of the Downs that, could I be but sure that my cell had an accessible window on the south, I would risk any crime, such as defying the lord of the manor, whose hand lies on it so heavily, shooting his deer, or pulling down one of his terrible 'Stick No Bills', if only I knew that I could gaze at long leisure on such a view.

George Aitchison: 'Sussex'

I am always reminded of a foreign town when I go to Petworth. The high walls that conceal the magnificent home of the great Lord, the art-treasures that are behind those walls, and the generous way in which these galleries are thrown open to the public, the narrow streets, somewhat overshadowed by tall houses, as if shelter from the hot sunshine had to be provided, the busy life of the market-place, the little cobbled way called Lombard Street, that curves so that you gain a view of the tall church-spire at the end, then the encircling walls, and the walks between walls on the outskirts of the little town, with here and there above them glimpses of the distant Downs - all these things give an atmosphere of something that we usually meet when we cross the Channel.

Viscountess Wolseley: 'Some Sussex Byways'

I myself think that Petworth is the prettiest town in the entire county. Its little streets are full of charming houses, Tudor and Georgian. But everything is overshadowed by THE house, the greatest and most beautiful mansion in Sussex.

Desmond Seward: 'Sussex'

The great house and its pictures are the proper sight in Petworth for the well-regulated traveller, but I went down steps into an old shop to buy a loaf, and across the market-place into another dark shop to buy a paper. It is a calm, compact little town with domesticity in the narrow streets, and cats sleeping among the aspidistras and lace curtains in the parlour windows at your elbow. The cottages lean at all angles and have white steps before them spanning the cobbled gutter by the roadside. The roofs undulate with age, and the chimney-stacks are a medley of surprising designs. And there are the larger red-brick houses with white pillared doorways, the genteel residences of two hundred years ago.

Walter Wilkinson: 'A Sussex Peepshow'

• Petworth House
(National Trust)
(01798) 342207
197: SU 976219

Some other Sussex houses
open to the public:

• Uppark
(National Trust)
(01730) 825415
197: SU 779177

• Stansted Park
(01705) 412265
197: SU 761104

• Goodwood House
(01243) 774107
197: SU 886088

• Parham House
(01903) 742021
197: TQ 060143

• Glynde Place
(01273) 858224
198: TQ 456093

• Firle Place
(01273) 858335
198: TQ 473072

A selection of smaller
historic houses:

• Hammerwood Park
(01342) 850594
187: TQ 442389

• Standen, East Grinstead
(National Trust)
(01342) 323029
187: TQ 389356

• Priest House, West Hoathly
(Sussex Archaeological
Society)
(01342) 810479
187: TQ 362326

• St Mary's, Bramber
(01903) 816205
198: TQ 189065

• Brickwall House &
Garden, Northiam
(01797) 223329
199: TQ 833239

There are times when we find ourselves responding with an 'Oh, come off it!' to Richard Jefferies, but his swooping spiritual flights are restrained by a tethering of observation and wildlife knowledge which earned him the respect of such fellow practitioners as Edward Thomas (who wrote his biography) and W.H. Hudson (who, while writing Nature in Downland, settled himself in the house where Jefferies had died, and later arranged to be buried close to his mentor in Broadwater Cemetery). Though not a Sussex man, Jefferies discovered the county at a young age, paid frequent visits (he wrote some of the autobiographical The Story of My Heart at Pevensey) and finally settled here with his wife and two children - living variously at Hove, Rotherfield, Crowborough and Goring. He died of consumption when he was only thirty eight.

Beachy Head, a grim place in a storm and a fatal lure to suicides (on average more than a dozen each year), is as glorious as Jefferies describes it when a warm breeze is blowing and the sky is blue. The Sussex Downs begin (or end) here, rising high above Eastbourne to the east and running west over miles of unspoilt, undulating countryside via Birling Gap and the Seven Sisters to Cuckmere Haven and beyond (see p. 18). On the way you pass the old Belle Tout lighthouse, now a private house: too often obscured by fog, it was replaced in 1902 by the pretty red and white tower which sits at the foot of Beachy Head and gives the great cliff an awesome perspective.

— Beachy Head —

LAND OF HEALTH

The little rules and little experiences, all the petty ways of narrow life, are shut off behind by the ponderous and impassable cliff; as if we had dwelt in the dim light of a cave but coming out at last to look at the sun, a great stone had fallen and closed the entrance, so that there was no return to the shadow. The impassable precipice shuts off our former selves of yesterday, forcing us to look out over the sea only, or up to the deeper heaven.

There are ledges three hundred feet above, and from these now and then a jackdaw glides out and returns again to his place, where, when still and with folded wings, he is but a speck of black. A spire of chalk still higher stands out from the wall, but the rains have got behind it and will cut the crevice deeper and deeper into its foundation. Water, too, has carried the soil from under the turf at the summit over the verge, forming brown streaks.

Upon the beach lies a piece of timber, part of a wreck; the wood is torn and the fibres rent where it was battered against the dull edge of the rocks. The heat of the sun burns, thrown back by the dazzling chalk; the river of ocean flows ceaselessly, casting the spray over the stones; the unchanged sky is blue.

Let us go back and mount the steps at the Gap, and rest on the sward there. I feel that I want the presence of grass. The sky is a softer blue, and the sun genial now the eye and the mind alike are relieved - the one of the strain of too great solitude (not the solitude of the woods), the other of too brilliant and hard a contrast of colours. Touch but the grass and the harmony returns; it is repose after exaltation.

On returning homewards towards Eastbourne, stay awhile by the tumulus on the slope. There are others hidden among the furze; butterflies flutter over them, and the bees hum round by day; by night the nighthawk passes, coming up from the fields and even skirting the sheds and houses below. The rains beat on them, and the storm drives the dead leaves over the low green domes; the waves boom on the shore far down.

How many times has the morning star shone yonder in the East? All the mystery of the sun and of the stars centres around these lowly mounds.

But the glory of these glorious Downs is the breeze. The air in the valleys immediately beneath them is pure and pleasant; but the least climb, even a hundred feet, puts you on a plane with the atmosphere itself, uninterrupted by so much as the tree-tops. It is air without admixture. If it comes from the south, the waves refine it; if inland, the wheat and flowers and grass distil it. The great headland and the whole rib of the promontory is wind-swept and washed with air; the billows of the atmosphere roll over it.

Discover some excuse to be up there always, to search for stray mushrooms - they will be stray, for the crop is gathered extremely early in the morning - or to make a list of flowers and grasses; to do anything, and if not, go always without any pretext. Lands of gold have been found, and lands of spices and precious merchandise; but this is the land of health.

Richard Jefferies: 'The Breeze on Beachy Head'

• Beachy Head Centre
(01323) 737273
199: TV 586956

• Beachy Head Lighthouse
199: TV 583951

• Belle Tout (private)
199: TQ 563955

See 'Old Mother Goring', p. 55, for other downland summits

See 'Duke William's Beacon' in Living Sussex; *'The Battle of Beachy Head' in* The Sussex Story

*Tourist Information, Eastbourne
(01323) 411400*

Where Richard Jefferies lived in Sussex (all private):

• *'The Downs',
London Road, Crowborough
(with plaque)
188: TQ 515315*

• *87 Lorna Road, Hove
198: TQ 295053*

• *Jefferies House,
Jefferies Lane (off Sea Lane),
Goring-by-Sea
198: TQ 112026*

Where Richard Jefferies is buried:

• *Broadwater Cemetery,
South Farm Road,
Worthing
198: TQ 143044*

LAMBS' TAILS AND OTHER DELICACIES

It's tempting to link the stolidity of the Sussex 'wunt be druv' countryman with the solidity of his diet. There are very few recipes with a Sussex tag, and every one of them seems designed to induce a heavy tread and a sluggish demeanour. As someone who loves to prepare pond pudding for his unsuspecting guests, I shall defend its delicious lemony stodginess to the last but, fashioned as it is from suet, flour, butter and sugar, it can hardly be termed a delicacy. Sussex plum heavies? Scones of a sort (those plums are raisins), but the name tells you all you really need to know. And swimmers? Suet again! Lambs' tails and thrushes must have been a welcome relief.

The wonder, considering such a one-dimensional culinary tradition, is that Sussex should have so many fine restaurants. (Few of them, of course, pretend to provide local fare - although English's, illustrated here, can at least offer fish caught in Channel waters). True to form, however, when one of them does at last create a dish that travels from Sussex around the world, what should it be but a heavy, sickly pudding. The Hungry Monk in Jevington has a deserved reputation for its subtle cooking, but proudly proclaims itself the inventor of that dieter's dread, banoffi pie: an improbable sludge of banana and condensed milk boiled to toffee in the tin.

Friends of mine, preparing this sweet for a dinner party but overcome by a sudden amorousness, descended to the kitchen some time later to find the condensed milk dripping from the ceiling. Just desserts.

> To make a Sussex pond pudding:
>
> Line a dish with suet dough, and place butter, sugar and a pricked lemon in the bottom of it. Seal with a lid of suet, and steam or boil for 2-3 hours.

The cabbage is the South Down peasant's favourite vegetable, and I really think that he would rather eat it cold than hot. I have known Sussex men and women who looked upon boiled cabbage, saturated with vinegar, as one of the greatest table luxuries possible. The women have yet to learn the art of cooking vegetables - their boiled cabbage is detestable, and the smell of it scents the cottage long after it has been consumed.

Arthur Beckett: 'The Spirit of the Downs'

Lambing time was another exciting time in our lives. While they were quite small their tails were cut off and were used to make pies. Very nice they were, too. Mother would pour hot water on them and all the wool came away easily.

Evelyn Pentecost: 'A Shepherd's Daughter'

> To make 'swimmers':
>
> Roll a piece of suet dough out to about half an inch thick. Cut into rounds the size of a saucer. Drop them into boiling water and cook quickly for about fifteen minutes. Remove with a skimmer. Fork the tops and add a dollop of butter and a spoonful of brown sugar.

Swimmers were a great joy when I stayed with my grandmother. She would make me one for my 'elevenses'. Just to think of them takes me back to a cottage garden, with me and my sister sitting on little wooden stools, pulling apart a swimmer floating in butter and a spoonful of brown sugar with an old-fashioned three-pronged fork.

Lillian Candlin: 'Memories of Old Sussex'

Birds, I've ate thousands of them: blackbirds and what we called greybirds, they were song thrushes. All that sort of thing. They'm jolly good, I tell you. Mother always used to make a pie of them. Like a game pie. You skin them, you don't pluck them. Skin the breast off, because there's nothing on them really, only the breast. Then put a nice pastry on top and pop them in the oven. But you need a couple of dozen birds for a good meal.

Gilbert Sargent: 'A Sussex Life'

And undoubtedly, Poet, you acquired in other countries a habit of eating that Gorgonzola cheese, which is made of soap in Connecticut; and Stilton, which is not made at Stilton; and Camembert, and other outlandish things. But in Sussex, let me tell you, we have but one cheese, the name of which is CHEESE. It is One; and undivided, though divided into a thousand fragments, and unchanging, though changing in place and consumption. There is in Sussex no Cheese but Cheese, and it is the same true Cheese from the head of the Eastern Rother to Harting Hill, and from the sea-beach to that part of Surrey which we gat from the Marches with sword and with bow. In colour it is yellow, which is the right colour of Cheese. It is neither young nor old. Its taste is that of Cheese, and nothing more. A man may live upon it all the days of his life.

Hilaire Belloc: 'The Four Men'

• *English's Oyster Bar,*
East Street, Brighton
(01273) 327980
198: TQ 312040

• *The Hungry Monk,*
Jevington
(01323) 482178
199: TQ 563016

Some of Bert Winborne's
story is told in my book The
Upstart Gardener, which
sprang from a radio series
we made together, but I've
never stopped learning
things about him - or from
him. Born in 1905, he sailed
into his cheerful nineties
with a creaking gardener's
knee his only infirmity, his
memory both as keen as his
trusty blade ('sharp knife,
sharp boy,' he'd say) and as
tangy as one of his deeply
coloured vats of liquid
manure. It's a rare man
who sifts the loam of his life
between calloused fingers
with such manifest content,
and a churlish one who asks
whether the class-bound
world in which he worked
wasn't unacceptable. Of
course I did ask it, in a
tentative fashion, and
received for my pains not a
flea in the ear but a proud
affirmation of the richness
of a gardener's life in those
days when teams of a dozen
or more sweated long and
hard to provide year-round
flowers and vegetables for
the big houses of Sussex.
Yes, the hours were long
and the pay was poor, but
you took a pride in what
you did - and your pride
was justified. Such love is
unanswerable. If I were able
to reorder the recent past
I would certainly enjoy
sorting out the aristocracy
and their country cousins,
but I would make sure to
preserve one great estate
where Bert could find happy
employment for the rest of
his days.
   Accent and dialect are
difficult to reproduce without
a false suggestion of naivety
or quaintness. Bert (who is
as shrewd as they come) has
the old Mid Sussex on his
tongue, and I would ask you
to hear it sounding through
the flat words on the page.

A GARDENER'S LIFE

I got up to Borde Hill just after the war, first war, as garden boy for
Mr and Mrs Stephenson Clarke. There was only three old
gentlemen there as gardeners then, but as the time went on new
men come in. I think they had nine or ten eventually. They had two
farms, and they had wood reeves to look after the rides and make
sure all the trees was in order. We had quite a lot of very rare
shrubs in the garden. In one big greenhouse we had a banana tree,
and the other end of it we had an orange tree. Not very big, but we
used to get them. Oranges used to be like a tangerine, and the old
bananas used to be those little finger bananas, about the size of
your finger, about nine or ten on a bunch.

   When you walked through them big gates of a morning it
seemed like you was entering another world, another world
entirely. Seven o'clock was seven o'clock, not a minute past. That's
when you started, and you used to have twenty minutes for
breakfast at eight. Took all your own grub, naturally. They didn't
give you anything, mate! An hour for lunch. Five o'clock you
knocked off, half past four Saturdays. And when you was walking
down the drive to go home in the evening, you felt proud that you
was part of all that.

   When all the planting out needed to be done in the spring,
the old head gardener used to say, 'Well, you'd better go home and
have a quick tea. I want you back here in half an hour.' You'd work
right through till it got dark. You didn't get anything extra for it.
And when your turn came for the weekend, perhaps every five
weeks, you got no money for that, either. It was all part of the job,
see. You knew that when you took it on. You didn't argue, by Jove
no! There was always someone outside the gate ready to take your
job. Money wasn't very good, but you stuck it and you done your
best. I'd like to see them old days back again, where you left school
and you went into building or plumbing or whatever it may be and
you had to do as you was told.

   You weren't allowed inside the big house. They wanted
you away from it as much as possible, out of sight. But as you got
on in the garden you got high enough that the head gardener
would trust you to go down to the house to get orders for the
vegetables for the day. You went to the window with your
vegetables, and everything had to be just so - washed, clean and
straight - or the old cook would very soon tell you what was wrong
with it. You had to be smart. You had to have a clean collar. You
hadn't got a tie - you couldn't afford one - but a nice clean shirt on
Mondays, and always clean boots. But the thing was, you only had
one pair of boots, and when you went home they was wet through.
I'd have my old boots in front of the hearth, drying, so I could get a
bit of polish on in the morning.

   You saw the lady and gentleman occasionally. If you was
working in the drive you generally stood up and just recognised
them as they went by. Not that they saw you probably, but that
was the regular thing to do. And if they come round the garden
you always disappeared somewhere behind a shrub. When they
came up to you, you generally used to raise your hat and talk to
them. A lot of the gardeners used to take their hat off and put it
underneath their arm. No, there wasn't no resentment. It was the

• Borde Hill Garden,
Haywards Heath
(01444) 450326
187/198: TQ 323266

For other High Weald
gardens see 'Kew in the
Country', p. 14

Some other Sussex gardens
open to the public:

• Denmans Garden,
Fontwell
(01243) 542808
197: SU 947071

• West Dean Gardens,
near Chichester
(01243) 811303
197: SU 862127

• Highdown Chalk Gardens,
near Worthing
(01903) 501054
198: TQ 097042

• Pashley Manor Gardens,
Ticehurst
(01580) 200692
188/199 TQ 706291

• Great Dixter (house and
garden), Northiam
(01797) 253160
188/199 TQ 818251

recognised thing you done that. And if you didn't do it the old head gardener wanted to know why you didn't do it, and you'd say you forgot. 'Well, you don't forget in *these* gardens.' Head gardener walked about with a nice suit on and a trilby hat, and occasionally he would put an apron on and do something in one of the greenhouses.

One turn, when I was at Bedales, another big estate, we had a new bloke come along, and he was a bit of a Labour guy. He started to cause a lot of trouble, and it wasn't long before he got outed. They shuffled *him* out. He was causing a bit of disturbance, because he'd be saying, when we was having our lunch or our dinner, that we shouldn't be doing this or that. Stirring it up, as we call it now. We were Conservatives. When I was still a young gardener and I'd moved on from Borde Hill to a place called Yarrow, a big house in Balcombe Road, Mrs Darcy Watson come round the garden one morning and said to the head gardener, 'I'd like to speak to Winborne.' And she said, 'Winborne, I've put you on the Junior Imperial League. I'd like you to attend regular and make notes of the meetings, and I would like to know the morning afterwards.' It was nothing to do with gardening. They wanted to know what was going on in the villages around, so that the Conservatives could be at the front of it. I couldn't afford a wallet, and I used to have an old broken pencil, and sometimes I used to take an envelope out of the dustbin, a clean envelope, and take it to the meetings, and I used to make one or two notes on the back of this envelope. One time there was something coming on at one of the big estates, and they needed stands to be put up, so they asked if our garden could supply trestles. 'I hope you said Yes, Winborne,' she said. 'I didn't say Yes, my lady, because I didn't know if I was entitled.' 'But of course, Winborne. Anything that's to do with the Conservatives, you say Yes.'

It was never the same after the second world war. The estates were broke up. Today there's only just a few big places left, and they're run by businesses. I'd love to have the old times back. They were good old days, and sometimes it makes me swallow to think that they're gone. Good old days!

Bert Winborne

AS SHE IS SPOKE

William Parish was one of those many well-born and highly-educated nineteenth century clerics who found that the life of a country parson allowed ample time for extra-ecclesiastical pursuits. Vicar of Selmeston with Alciston from 1863 until his death forty one years later, Parish wrote books on various subjects, but it's for a work first published in 1875 that later generations are in his debt: A Dictionary of the Sussex Dialect and Collection of Provincialisms in Use in the County of Sussex.

The italicised entries here (a selection from A to F) give an idea of Parish's range and sense of humour, while the extract from his preface sets out his stall: this is to be no sneering derision of peasant idiocies (albeit that a chuckle is frequently in order) but an investigation as scientifically accurate as circumstances will allow: many of the entries have an e, m or w alongside them to indicate that they are to be heard in East, Mid or West Sussex and, sure enough, I have found that many a word used by Bert Winborne (p. 74) has an m beside it. But Parish was well aware, too, that his work should be entertaining: 'I confess that I was much surprised when I found that one of the first pieces of advice which was circulated among the members of the English Dialect Society was to abstain from etymology. It seemed to me that to encourage people to collect words, and at the same time to forbid them to attempt to give their derivations, was very like presenting a boy with a pair of skates and then desiring him on no account to go upon the ice.'

ADONE. Leave off. I am told on good authority that when a Sussex damsel says 'Oh! do adone,' she means you to go on; but when she says 'Adone-do,' you must leave off immediately.

In almost every establishment in the country there is to be found some old groom, or gardener, bailiff or factotum, whose odd expressions and quaint sayings and apparently outlandish words afford a never-failing source of amusement to the older as well as to the younger members of the household, who are not aware that many of the words and expressions which raise the laugh are purer specimens of the English language than the words which are used to tell the story in which they are introduced. Every page of this dictionary will show how distinctly the British, Roman, Saxon and Norman elements are to be traced in the words in everyday use among our labouring people, who retain among them many of the oldest forms of old words which, although they have long ago become obsolete among their superiors in education, are nevertheless still worthy of our respect and attention. Like the old coins which he so often turns up with his plough, the words of the Sussex labourer bear a clear stamp of days long past and gone and tell a story of their own.

Rev. W.D. Parish: 'A Dictionary of the Sussex Dialect'

BAWL. To read aloud. A mother said of a child who did not go to school on account of illness, 'I keeps him to his book all the same, and his father likes to hear him bawl a bit in the evening.'

1. Lookee, you be purty, my love, lookee, you be purty. You've got dove's eyes adin yer locks; yer hair is lik a flock of goats dat appear from Mount Gilead.
2. Yer teeth be lik a flock of ship just shared, dat come up from de ship-wash; every one of em bears tweens, an nare a one among em is barren.
3. Yer lips be lik a thread of scarlet, an yer speech is comely; yer temples be lik a bit of a pomegranate adin yer locks.

Mark Antony Lower: 'A Sussex Version of the Song of Solomon'

As a youngster I heard dialect and old-fashioned slang words and phrases used all the time, as I think my family were fairly slow to react to modern trends. Even today I find myself using words like spruser for someone who is a bit of a con man, or dorm when I actually mean to move slowly and clumsily. Somehow the standard words seem so much less descriptive than the old words I was brought up with. Although I would hesitate to use them in normal conversation, I can remember with satisfaction my parents coming out with scores of such words, such as dinlow (slow-witted), clung (half-dry), kiddie (mate or work-fellow) and puckered (snatched with cold).

Tony Wales: 'Sussex - Customs, Curiosities & Country Lore'

CONCERNED IN LIQUOR. Drunk. This is one of the many expressions used in Sussex to avoid the word drunk. To have had a little beer, means to have had a great deal too much; to have half-a-pint otherwhile, means to be an habitual drunkard; to be none the better for what he had took, means to be much the worse; to be noways tossicated, implies abject helplessness. A Sussex man may be tight, or concerned in liquor, but drunk never!

In the village of Selmeston the blacksmith's shop is next door to the public-house. I have met numbers of people going up to the forge, but never one going to the Barley-mow.

In losing your way in this neighbourhood do not ask the passer-by for Selmeston, but for Simson; for Selmeston, pronounced as it is spelt, does not exist. Sussex men are curiously intolerant of the phonetics of orthography. Brightelmstone was called Brighton from the first, although only in the last century was the spelling modified to agree with the sound. Chalvington (the name of a village north of Selmeston) is a pretty word, but Sussex declines to call it other than Chawton; Firle becomes Furrel; Lewes is almost Lose, but not quite; Heathfield is Hefful.

E.V. Lucas: 'Highways and Byways in Sussex'

DARKS. A word used by sailors, but more particularly by smugglers, to signify those nights when the moon does not appear. In former times everyone in the agricultural districts of Sussex within reach of the coast was more or less connected with smuggling.

On one occasion a person had been deputed to inquire for 'Mr Pocock of Alciston' and, meeting a labourer near the place in question, he asked him if he could point out the residence of the individual. 'Noa,' was the reply; 'never heerd an 'im, an' doant know no sich place.' It afterwards turned out that the labourer was no other than Mr Pocock himself! 'Why,' said he, when the true nature of the inquiry dawned upon him, 'you should ha' axed fur Mus Palk of Ahson.'

Arthur Beckett: 'The Spirit of the Downs'

END-ON. In a great hurry. 'He went at it end-on, as though he meant to finish afore he begun.'

In my early days Sussex was rich with its own grammar and dialect. All words that ended in 'st' were given a double plural. At that time there was a popular ditty often quoted by parents and teachers in an effort to check this fault. It went:

> *I saw three ghosteses sitting on posteses,*
> *Eating hot toasteses.*
> *The butter ran down their fisteses,*
> *Dirty little beasteses.*

In the spring of 1980 I was standing at a bus stop near Ringmer. Waiting along with me was a countryman. As is usual with such men he started a conversation. To my delight, he said 'Days be drawing out.' Then, pointing to a tree, he continued: 'I sees the birdies be building their nesteses.'

I could have hugged him! It was wonderful to hear again someone speaking my Sussex.

Lillian Candlin: 'Memories of Old Sussex'

FARISEES. Fairies. By an unfortunate use of the reduplicated plural, the Sussex country people confuse the ideas of fairies and Pharisees in a most hopeless manner. A belief in fairies is by no means extinct in the South Downs districts.

Where Rev. W.D. Parish is buried:
* *Selmeston churchyard 199: TQ 510069*

Firle Beacon from the painting by Eric Ravilious 1930

Flint. The very name has the shine and sharpness of the thing itself. Yet this durable quartz lies in bands among the softest rock imaginable, chalk. There's an improbability, too, about its origins: the skeletal remains of soft under-sea sponges. Prehistoric man valued the sharp edges it gave his tools and weapons, but our theme is the tough beauty of a traditional flint wall. Can anyone visit West Dean in East Sussex, a village which seems to have pushed itself up out of the chalk and disdainfully shaken the white dust from its shoulders (our cover shows the thirteenth century rectory), without rejoicing in its lively mosaic of sturdy flintwork? Yet although we see such walls everywhere within carter's haul of the Downs and sea, there seem to have been no hymns sung in their praise - which is why I have felt obliged to write one myself.

The flints are found rough and jagged in the fields, softly rounded by the sea's pounding along the shore. 'They have been used, worked and unworked,' writes Jacquetta Hawkes in A Land, 'in every kind of building from pigsties to cathedrals.' True, but the humble use predominates, which is why the late eighteenth century Goodwood House, designed by James Wyatt for the third Duke of Richmond, is so surprising. The estate incorporates the famous racecourse in its lovely downland setting. I know nothing about horses and rarely chance a wager, but on a fine summer's day at Glorious Goodwood - 'a garden party with racing tacked on,' Edward VII said - soaking up the atmosphere is quite enough.

THE GIFT OF THE CHALK

By Sussex Downs our every squint
Will find thy colours all displayed
(White, blue, slate-grey, the sunlit hint
Of many another subtle shade,
A heart with glossy black inlaid)
In lovely walls, harlequinade!
Scarce barn, church, dovecote antique-made
But has thy lilting poetry in't.
      Knapped and squared,
      Round, unprepared
      And roughly layered:
Gift of the chalk for those who're skint,
Thy praises I shall never stint
Oh various, lightsome, steel-hard flint!

Goodwood House

At Goodwood where the horses sprint
The great lord might have had his pick
(Since, frankly, he was worth a mint
And kept his place in perfect nick,
Nor ever bought a thing on tick)[1]
Of polished stone or Flemish brick,
Egyptian marble[2] five feet thick -
But chose instead thy homely glint.
        And when poor Wyatt
        Threatened a riot,[3]
        Growled: 'Just try it:
For Sèvres, Louis Quinze and aquatint,[4]
A private showing of Peer Gynt,[5]
Are poor things next to Sussex flint!'

In Westmeston where wild flowers print
Their shadows on my garden wall
(Ivy, bramble, cuckoo pint)
Some damn-fool rector gave the call
To weed the greenery, roots and all,
(The boundary's part parochial)
Till the topmost stones began to fall -
And yet the church itself, by dint
        Of standing tough
        Ages enough
        (Be praised, thy stuff)
Proclaims we'll need no truss or splint:
By candle, bell and Septuagint,
There's nothing lasts like Sussex flint!

David Arscott: 'A Hymn to Flint'

• Goodwood House
(01243) 774107
197: SU 886088

See p. 69 for other Sussex houses open to the public

• The Rectory, West Dean
(cover picture)
199: TV 525996

Other examples of flint buildings at:

• Weald & Downland Open Air Museum, Singleton
(01243) 811348
197: SU 875128

See The Sussex Story for prehistoric flint mines

• Goodwood Racecourse
(01243) 774107
racedays: (01243) 774838
197: SU 884110

Other Sussex racecourses:

• Fontwell
(01243) 543335
197: SU 946067

• Brighton
(01273) 603580
198: TQ 332053

• Plumpton
(01273) 890383
198: TQ 362158

Notes on the second stanza:

[1] This seems to overstate the case, since the Duke's new building (an intended octagonal extension of the existing house) had to be abandoned less than half way through when the cash ran out.

[2] An unlikely material. The author perhaps has in mind the columns of the fireplace in the main entrance hall.

[3] This won't do: there is no evidence whatsoever that Wyatt resisted the use of flint.

[4] A demonstration of the depths to which a versifier will sink in the pursuit of rhyme. Sèvres porcelain and Louis XV furniture are, indeed, among the outstanding treasures at Goodwood, but the mention of aquatints is ludicrous in view of the fine collection of oil paintings, including masterpieces by Van Dyck.

[5] Ditto, and impossible. Ibsen's poetic drama, for which Grieg wrote the music, was written sixty years after the Duke's death.

QUIET AND SLY

We have a tremendous sense of humour in Sussex, although strangers may not always be aware of it. Our humour is of the quiet, sly kind that sneaks up on you when you are least expecting it, often by a neat sting in the end of a story. Our humorists usually operate with a perfectly serious expression and this makes the shock of being 'kidded' even greater. We don't go in for huge belly laughs; a grin or a chuckle is the most you will normally get out of a true Sussex countryman.

Tony Wales: 'A Sussex Garland'

The downland people's sense of humour is of the trivial order; the best expressions of the quality are nearly always unconscious. They will repeat a joke that is really no joke at all, until the repetition becomes irritating and almost nauseating. On a certain summer evening I filled my pipe in a village inn which was full of rustics. Some of the tobacco, not being sufficiently pressed down, hung over the side of the bowl, whereupon a labourer exclaimed, 'I say, mister, your pipe dribbles!' This was greeted by the company with a great roar of laughter, and references to the pipe that 'dribbled' were made at fairly regular intervals throughout the evening; and when I left I was bidden farewell with, 'Good night, sir; and mind your pipe don't dribble.'

Arthur Beckett: 'The Spirit of the Downs'

Perhaps the following tale may be a 'chestnut' to some, but it was related to me in three places many miles apart, and may be recorded in print as a typical example of quiet Sussex humour.

Old Father Wuzzel had just finished breakfast and was going to market. 'Now, Albe,' he said to his son, ''tis time us med a start; goo an' fetch th' hoss in.' Albe rose. 'Which hoss d'ye want today?' he asked 'Oh, fetch th' old 'un,' said his father; 'may's well wear th' old 'un out first, reckon.' Whereupon Albe sat down on his chair again and replied, 'You goo an' fetch 'un in then!'

Barclay Wills: 'Downland Treasure'

As an illustration of the long life which awaits a bit of real humour in our quiet country districts, I have heard just lately the following story told twice, and by persons so far removed from each other that the tradition of the anecdote is evidently preserved not only in but beyond the parish which gave it birth.

About ninety years ago the Vicar of Burwash was one Archdeacon Courtail, whose name was locally pronounced

---

We English take a peculiar pride in our sense of humour, but it's unlikely that the old Sussex countryman gave it much thought. The odd village wag may have burnished his anecdotes until they shone like horse brasses, but ribs were generally tickled in a more unassuming fashion. However unsophisticated the wit may have been, however, I can't help feeling that when poor Arthur Beckett left his downland pub, manfully stifling pangs of nausea, the joke was on him. I certainly chuckle to myself whenever I think of that dribbling pipe - and I'm sitting merrily with the raucous company in the snug, not striding outside with Arthur, nose in the air.

At times the humour dives deep and surfaces as thinly veiled contempt. In his Recollections of a Sussex Parson, Edward Boys Ellman (a rector of Berwick), reports the comment of a prisoner being sentenced to a long period of transportation: 'Thank you, my lord, and I hope that you may sit there till I come back again.'

In similar vein, Tony Wales recalls (in A Sussex Garland) 'a certain professional gentleman who had the habit of leaving his office at odd times during the afternoon and arriving home unexpectedly, in the hope of catching his gardener out in some misdeed. On one of these occasions he said to the gardener, in his usual gruff voice, "I hope you are planting those potatoes well apart!" "Y-yes," replied the fellow, "s-some in your garden and s-some in m-mine!"'

A line like that would be worth getting the sack for.

Kirtle. One Sunday afternoon a man, not quite sober, had strayed into the church and, hearing some sentence in the sermon which, in his half-drunken state, he thought was meant for himself, he called out: 'Don't rub too hard, Kirtle.'

The utterance was allowed to pass unnoticed, but shortly afterwards, the sentence being unfortunately repeated, the unhappy man again called out: 'Don't rub too hard, Kirtle; I told you not to rub too hard.'

This renewed interruption could not be overlooked, and the Archdeacon accordingly stopped, and requested the churchwardens to remove the man from the church. The request was obeyed, and as the irreverent offender was being led through the west door he stammered forth the still remembered sentence: 'Well, I never got into any trouble yet but what I always found friends to help me out.'

John Coker Egerton: 'Sussex Folk and Sussex Ways'

'Afore' is often used for 'before'. In East Dean, in East Sussex, Dan, a gardener, used it and when he said it in rich Sussex dialect it sounded marvellous. Dan also had the Sussex wit. One day when I was starting out for a country walk the weather looked 'quizzby' (unsettled) and I asked Dan if it was going to rain. 'Well,' he replied, 'it won't rain afore you gets back.' It poured with rain, and when I got back I said to him: 'You said it wasn't going to rain.' 'No, I didn't. I said it wouldn't afore you got back, but you didn't get back soon enough.'

Lillian Candlin: 'Memories of Old Sussex'

When all the seed was safely in the ground the next job was to try to keep it there, and that was not always as easy as it may sound. It was all very well to sing:

> *The man with his seed-lip he'll scatter the corn,*
> *Then the harrows will bury it to keep it from harm*

but five or six hundred sooty, ragged-winged robbers, from the rookery in the neighbouring village of Stanmer over the hill, had completely opposite views. They used to fly down daily in droves at this time of year to raid the freshly sown fields. This was an annual hazard and, although there was a small colony of rooks in the trees in the Dene garden overlooking the pond, by far the biggest dangers came from the rapacious 'Stanmer Park' rooks who outnumbered the 'Rottingdeaners' by about ten to one. Following a particularly fierce March gale, old Sham the bookie said, 'Blow, I should think that did blow. That blew all the feathers off the Stanmer Park rooks and I'm baggered if they didn't 'ave to walk 'ome.'

Bob Copper: 'A Song for Every Season'

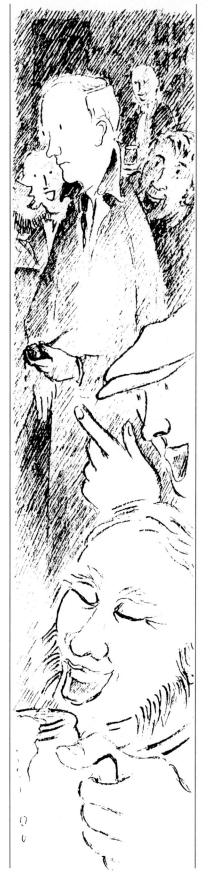

81

In ancient times the city was a refuge from the wilderness beyond its walls, a place of culture and refinement, sufficient unto itself - a noble ideal so besmirched by modern squalor, overcrowding and widespread deprivation that we now flock to the countryside for our health and sanity. Having made that journey myself, I may be accused of rosy-tinted vision in praising Lewes to the skies, but I have lived in different parts of it over several years, can still reach it in ten minutes by car and regard it as my own beloved 'civitas'. True, it lacks some amenities (the cinema in Eve Garnett's Lewes-based children's story has gone) and it sprawls a little at the edges, but it retains its heart intact and (as these writers testify) has a beauty of both character and setting. It has, moreover, its own castle, little theatre and brewery, and is generally the best advertisement that I know for the pleasures of urban living.

'Hunt the mathematical tiles' makes a challenging pastime for anyone taking a stroll through Lewes. These M-tiles, as the initiated like to call them, can be found on more than sixty of its buildings, in red, less commonly black and, rarely, yellow (which the cognoscenti prefer to call white) - a figure rivalled in England only by Brighton, a few miles away. Designed to mimic bricks (and they sometimes fool even the experts), they were in vogue in the Georgian period when timber-framed buildings were regarded as crude and unfinished: a softwood boarding was fixed to the wall and the tiles were then nailed to it and bedded in lime putty.

THE CAPITAL OF SUSSEX

Lewes is the capital of Sussex. Administratively, of course, it is the capital of East Sussex only, but that is merely an official device to save too much travelling. Lewes belongs to the whole of Sussex, and the whole of Sussex belongs to it. It is emphatically *the* county town. It is the epitome - and yet something of the inspiration - of all that Sussex is.

George Aitchison: 'Sussex'

Lewes has for me a twofold appeal. There is the old town itself, bestraddling its chalky crest and spilling down the slopes, with its abundant legacy of flint, tiles and brick. And then there is the setting, of which surely the fortunate citizens never grow tired: that glorious downland landscape with the clean lines of the hills silhouetted against the sky.

Alec Clifton-Taylor: 'Six More English Towns'

You can see Lewes lying like a box of toys under a green amphitheatre of chalk hills. On the whole it is set down better than any town I have seen in England.

William Morris

Scarcely anything at Lewes has been spoilt.

Nikolaus Pevsner: 'The Buildings of England - Sussex'

Not far from the coast, where the land suddenly becomes bare and chalky and folds itself into humps and hollows; where the wind from the south-west often tastes salt, and a herring-gull on the roof-tops is no uncommon sight, stands a Little Town. Some of it is very old and some of it was being built yesterday, but old and new, it is all of it built on the humps and hollows of bare hills so that whenever the inhabitants wish to go shopping, attend church, visit the cinema or even call on their friends, they must go up a hill and down a hill and often up and down again - sometimes several times over, which is all very well for the young and active but not such fun for the old and infirm.

Eve Garnett: 'In and Out and Roundabout'

Few people would dispute that it is one of the best looking small towns in the south of England, maybe in the whole country. Its main street is nearly a mile long and steps up from the river Ouse in a long and graceful slope, very slightly curving, but running more or less east to west. All the way up this High Street on either side there are fine houses.

Barbara Willard: 'Chichester and Lewes'

Among its unique features are the twittens. These narrow and winding lanes with their flint walls have been designed with ancient skill to anticipate and exclude such disruptive elements as the motor car. Their peace and quiet are in striking contrast to the High Street bustle and they provide many a useful short cut for the town's pedestrians, still a flourishing breed in a town surrounded by downland with its constant invitation to take to foot.

Peter Linklater: 'Lewes Twittens'

• *Lewes Castle & Barbican House Museum*
(Sussex Archaeological Society)
(01273) 474379
198: TQ 414101

Tourist Information, Lewes
(01273) 483448

See 'A Penny Loaf to Feed Old Pope', p. 46, for Bonfire Night in Lewes

— Lewes —

Atrocious verse, ridiculous plots, cardboard characters - the tipteerers, or mummers, plays that have survived in various parts of Sussex, and which diehards still perform in pubs at Christmas time, are wonderful knock-about stuff. The characters who introduce themselves with the vainglorious 'In Comes I' include King or Saint George (the alternatives speak volumes), Old Father Christmas, the Turkish Knight and Beelzebub. Yet, as Lillian Candlin reminds us, the original medieval version (a tale of St George fighting the heathens), 'had a deep spiritual meaning, symbolising the death and resurrection of the good earth'.

Readers with a sour and curmudgeonly attitude to Christmas had better ignore these pages. (And they certainly won't look out for Shaun Payne's flavoursome anthology, A Sussex Christmas, which I strongly recommend to addicts). For me - and, I suspect, for the writers represented here - there is always magic in the air. Sheila Kaye-Smith, who built a Roman Catholic church in the grounds of her East Sussex home, wrote several novels with a Wealden setting: how not fall in love with coy Bessie, singing carols in the frosty night? Vera Pragnell bought two derelict (and still surviving) cottages near Storrington in 1923 and founded a commune of fellow spirits, who read poetry, reared goats and hens, sang round campfires, lived in wooden huts painted with futuristic designs - and scandalised those who disapproved of their sexual laxity. Cowfold Monastery, as a map shows, was quite a traipse away in the Christmas darkness.

'IN COMES I !'

In comes I, King George,
That man of courage bold.
With my broad sword and spear
I have won ten tons of gold.
I fought the fiery dragon
And brought it to great slaughter,
And by that means I wish to win
The King of Egypt's daughter.
Neither unto thee will I bow nor bend -
Stand off! stand off!
I will not take you to be my friend.

West Wittering tipteerers play

I never saw a Christmas tree before, and enjoyed it like a child. It was far prettier than I expected. Four fir trees, two very large and two small, in big pots covered with gold apples and silver pears and every kind of pink, blue and green cornucopias filled with bon-bons.

Lucy Hare, writing to her sister, after seeing the first
Christmas tree in Sussex at Herstmonceux Place in 1843

Our only party on winter evenings was having all the children of the workmen to tea. They arrived shy and solemn, their faces shining with much application of yellow soap, and their hair sleekly greased - probably with lard. We could not blame them, for in the sixties we all used 'pomatum', but ours came from the hairdressers, scented and in coloured glass pots. Tea in the kitchen wore off some of the shyness of our guests and then came games in the schoolroom, such as 'Hunt the slipper', when a little impromptu conversation between cobbler and customer was received as exquisite wit. To finish there was a Christmas tree, and what a simple and inexpensive joy it was! A home-made garment for each, pinafore, hood or scarf, a bag of marbles, a penny Dutch doll gaily dressed, with a few bags of sweets, and coloured candles.

One year we sought to make a variation by putting the gifts in the sack of a very mild version of Father Christmas, but it was not a success. The unsophisticated little natives who had never seen or heard of fancy dress took him for a bogey of the worst description and yelled with terror, in spite of the buxom cook's explaining 'It is only Master Louis inside!' So next year we went back to the Christmas tree which they knew and loved.

Maude Robinson: 'A South Down Farm in the Sixties'

Then winter came, with carol-singing, and the choristers tramped round, lantern-led, from farm to farm. There in the fluttering light outside Kitchenhour, Old Turk, Ellenwhorne, or Edzell, Robert would watch Bessie's chicory-flower eyes under her hood, while the steam of their breath mingled in the frosty air, and they drooped their heads together, singing to each other, only to each other, Good King Wenceslas, As Joseph was A-walking, or In the Fields with the Flocks.

Sheila Kaye-Smith: 'Sussex Gorse'

Much of the fare now connected with Christmas but eaten all the year round did not appear until Christmas in those days. Up to the 1920s oranges were only in season from early December until early April. The only place in the days before refrigeration that sent oranges to England was Spain. At Christmas these were very sour. So much so that we were allowed to poke a hole in the skins and into the hole push a lump of sugar. The juice was then sucked through the sugar. There was no bottled or tinned orange juice, so oranges were definitely a large part of Christmas, and every child hoped to see an orange sticking out at the top of their stocking.

Lillian Candlin: 'Memories of Old Sussex'

Christmas was wonderful. I seldom enter churches and have come to use the term *Christianity* very warily and seldom, so far removed seem Churches and Christianities from the daring spirit of Christ. But on Christmas Eve I went to the Monastery's Midnight Mass and knelt at the Cradle of the Holy Child and, coming home, got completely and utterly lost! Never, surely, was a lost thing happier than I: the Mass music rang in my ears, haunting and beautiful, and the night was deliciously frosty and pitch dark. The cold wind blew in my face, defying sleepiness, and every now and again a frightened bird would fly up, screeching, as I plodded on, up hill and down dale, my foot slipping into bunny-holes, my arms striking against trees. Once it was the howl of a fox that broke the silence of that amazing night. And never a sign of a dwelling and not one guiding star! Towards dawn I came to a cottage and its red-bearded cowman-owner insisted on accompanying me all the way back, many miles, to my caravan-home.

'You seemed such a chit of a child,' he said gently, 'and my girl's across the Sea and I'd like to think someone would do the same for her.'

So we drank hot cocoa in the van and he tucked me up with clumsy tenderness as we wished each other Happy Christmasses.

Vera G. Pragnell: 'The Story of the Sanctuary'

Where Sheila Kaye-Smith lived:
• *Doucegrove (private, with her church close by)*
199: TQ 827216

• *Sleepy Hollow (formerly The Sanctuary), Heath Common, near Storrington*
198: TQ 112144

• *Cowfold Monastery*
198: TQ 206208

*And so, finally, to Hilaire
Belloc. The similarities and
contrasts with Kipling are
striking. Both men were
outsiders who fell in love
with Sussex, although
Belloc (born in 1870, and so
five years the junior) came
to it earlier in life. Both
knew tragedy (Kipling
losing a son in the first
world war, and also a
daughter; Belloc losing a
son in each of the two wars,
and his wife when he was
only thirty-four). Both
wrote copiously about their
adopted county. Their
personalities, on the other
hand, were very different.
Kipling is remembered by
those who worked for him at
Bateman's as decent but
somewhat remote (his little
American wife was
formidable), whereas it's
easy to imagine meeting
Belloc over a pint and
staying on until closing
time. 'The names of the inns
of Sussex are scattered
through Belloc's books like
holy places for the pilgrims
of an irreligious age,' as
Bernard Smith says in
Writers in Sussex. And not
inns, only: Belloc was a
compulsive list-maker,
telling the places he loved
like beads on a rosary. The
Four Men, that quirky,
boisterous, semi-fictional
account of a journey on foot
across Sussex (see p. 58), is
gloriously packed with them.*

*Belloc spent the last forty-
seven years of his life at
King's Land in Shipley, a
former tithe barn become a
rambling house and lit only
by candles and oil-lamps.
With it came a working
windmill, the prettiest in
Sussex, which is open once
a month during the season.
Belloc, a memorial plaque
tells us, 'garnered a harvest
of wisdom and sympathy for
young and old'. Amen.*

THE SOUTH COUNTRY

When I am living in the Midlands
    That are sodden and unkind,
I light my lamp in the evening:
    My work is left behind;
And the great hills of the South Country
    Come back into my mind.

The great hills of the South Country
    They stand along the sea;
And it's there walking in the high woods
    That I could wish to be,
And the men that were boys when I was a boy
    Walking along with me.

The men that live in West England
    They see the Severn strong,
A-rolling on rough water brown
    Light aspen leave along.
They have the secret of the Rocks,
    And the oldest kind of song.

But the men that live in the South Country
    Are the kindest and most wise,
They get their laughter from the loud surf,
    And the faith in their happy eyes
Comes surely from our Sister the Spring
    When over the sea she flies;
The violets suddenly bloom at her feet,
    She blesses us with surprise.

I never get between the pines
    But I smell the Sussex air;
Nor I never come on a belt of sand
    But my home is there.
And along the sky the line of the Downs
    So noble and so bare.

A lost thing I could never find,
    Nor a broken thing mend:
And I fear I shall be all alone
    When I get towards the end.
Who will there be to comfort me
    Or who will be my friend?

I will gather and carefully make my friends
    Of the men of the Sussex Weald,
They watch the stars from silent folds,
    They stiffly plough the field.
By them and the God of the South Country
    My poor soul shall be healed.

If I ever become a rich man,
    Or if ever I grow to be old,
I will build a house with deep thatch
    To shelter me from the cold,
And there shall the Sussex songs be sung
    And the story of Sussex told.

Hilaire Belloc: 'The South Country'

• *Shipley Windmill*
& King's Land (private)
198: TQ 143218

Earlier Belloc homes:

• *Bleak House, Top Road,*
Slindon (private, with plaque)
197: TQ 962083
• *Courthill Farmhouse,*
Slindon (private)
197: TQ 960089

Where Belloc is buried:
• *Church of Our Lady of*
Consolation, West Grinstead
198: TQ 177212

For other Sussex mills
see <u>The Sussex Story</u>

— Shipley Mill —

DIGGING DEEPER

So many books have been written about Sussex that most have the longevity of September butterflies. Although some of the more recent are detailed in the Acknowledgements, others mentioned in these pages will be unearthed only by ransacking library shelves or (a pleasurable pursuit) following their musty scent into the inner recesses of second-hand bookshops.

They are not recommended equally, of course. Kipling is the master, the one writer of the first rank to make Sussex a recurring theme. Sussex: A Kipling Anthology, *compiled by Rosemary Mitchell and Joan M. Vann (Padda Books) is an excellent short introduction to the poetry, while readers not familiar with the short stories should perhaps begin with the haunting* They, *in which the motorist narrator rattles through the countryside in the manner of his creator.*

Belloc has to be mentioned in the next breath, and The Four Men *is essential reading for its vigour, its sheer fun and, especially, its sense of place. Bob Copper, whose* Early to Rise, A Song for Every Season *and* Songs and Southern Breezes *are pre-eminent among late twentieth century Sussex literature, has tramped the lanes and manfully endured what the inns have to offer in order to write* Across Sussex With Belloc *(Alan Sutton) - a loving reprise of that work.*

My selection is personal and makes no pretence of comprehensiveness, but every generation needs its fresh compilation. Although Margaret Goldsworthy's Sussex Bedside Anthology *of 1950 is full of good things, and ranges further back in time than has suited my project, tastes have inevitably changed. The leisurely style common during the first half of the century, for example, seems by turns quirky and ponderous, civilised and pompous, although the prose has generally dated less disastrously than the verse. Yet those writers, assuming an audience which knew little about the county, were at least able to recount colourful travellers' tales. Their modern successors are for the most part condemned to produce characterless guide books, only a few managing to rise above the prevailing flatness. Here I include my friend Ben Darby, who died while this volume was in preparation: his three books,* View of Sussex, The South Downs *and* Journey Through the Weald, *draw on a lifetime's exploration of our towns and countryside.*

Those who enjoy folklore and ancient customs, given but little room in these pages, will find plenty to their taste in the books by Tony Wales, among them A Sussex Garland *(Godfrey Cave Associates), and Lillian Candlin, whose* Tales of Old Sussex *and* Memories of Old Sussex *are published by Countryside Books. In similar vein, The Rev. W.D. Parish's* A Dictionary of the Sussex Dialect, *expanded by Helena Hall and published by Gardner's in 1957, is hugely entertaining. Another reissued classic,* The Diary of Thomas Turner *(edited by David Vaisey) was published by OUP in 1984 and in paperback by CTR ten years later.*

I have smuggled a little information about writers into the margins but, since my intention has been to celebrate Sussex rather than to do justice to individual authors, many of those who have lived and worked here make no appearance at all: Robert Tressell, who set The Ragged Trousered Philanthropists *in Hastings, leaps immediately to mind, and readers will doubtless have their own regrets. Several books come to our rescue here, however, among them* Writers in Sussex *by Bernard Smith and Peter Haas (Redcliffe), and* Writers in Romney Marsh *by Ian Finlayson (Severn House). Guides to the Bloomsbury set include Judy Moore's* The Bloomsbury Trail in Sussex *(S.B. Publications) and Millie Collins's booklet* Bloomsbury in Sussex *(Albourne Publications).*

A list of Sussex booklets would require several pages, but the working class autobiographies published by QueenSpark in Brighton make an impressive list, while Susan Rowland of Offham, near Lewes, is also producing a useful series of otherwise unsung 'lives'.

And finally, a magazine. The best libraries stock bound volumes of the old Sussex County Magazine, *which are packed with fascinating and wide-ranging material. Now* Downs Country, *first published in the autumn of 1994, seems set to establish itself as similarly invaluable 'for those' (to quote its strapline) 'who love the Downland and Weald'.*

GAZETTEER OF SITES

*Although you will need seven Ordnance Survey Landranger
1: 50 000 maps for the whole of Sussex (see inside covers),
numbers 197-199 include everything except the northern and
eastern extremities. The gazetteer lists sites in order of first
appearance in the right-hand margins.*

Map 186:
*Aldershot, Guildford & surrounding area
(this covers a small area of north-west Sussex)*

Kirdford Church ....(Sussex marble)	TQ 018265	....p 29
Drunkenness plaque, Kirdford..............	TQ 018266	....p 33
Aldworth, Black Down........(Tennyson)	SU 926309	....p 45
Lurgashall Church...............(Tennyson)	SU 938273	....p 45

Map 187:
*Dorking, Reigate and CRAWLEY area (also covering
HORSHAM and EAST GRINSTEAD)*

Crabbet Park, Worth......(Scawen Blunt)	TQ 305373	....p 11
Wakehurst Place, Ardingly	TQ 339314	....p 15
Nymans Garden, Handcross..................	TQ 265294	....p 15
High Beeches Garden, Handcross..........	TQ 278307	....p 15
Leonardslee Gardens, Lower Beeding ..	TQ 222259	....p 15
Borde Hill Garden, Haywards Heath....	TQ 323266	....p 15,75
King & Barnes Brewery, Horsham........	TQ 168307	....p 33
The Hawth, Crawley	TQ 278362	....p 61
Ashdown Forest Visitor Centre.............	TQ 433324	....p 63
Hammerwood Park.................................	TQ 442389	....p 69
Standen, East Grinstead........................	TQ 389356	....p 69
Priest House, West Hoathly	TQ 362326	....p 69

Map 188:
*Maidstone & the Weald of Kent (including CROWBOROUGH,
MAYFIELD and the WADHURST/TICEHURST area)*

Bodiam Castle	TQ 785256	....p 57
A.A. Milne/E.H. Shepard memorial	TQ 468320	....p 63
Poohsticks Bridge	TQ 470338	....p 63
Mayfield Church.....................................	TQ 586270	....p 67
The Old Palace, Mayfield	TQ 587271	....p 67
Broadreed Farm........(ancient landscape)	TQ 548253	....p 67
'The Downs', Crowborough .....(Jefferies)	TQ 515315	....p 71
Pashley Manor Gardens, Ticehurst..........	TQ 706291	....p 75
Great Dixter, Northiam............................	TQ 818251	....p 75

Map 189:
Ashford & Romney marsh area (for RYE and WINCHELSEA)

Lamb House, Rye	TQ 920202	....p 7
The Black Boy, Rye.......(Radclyffe Hall)	TQ 922204	....p 7
The Forecastle, Rye.......(Radclyffe Hall)	TQ 922203	....p 7
The Mermaid Inn, Rye	TQ 921204	....p 7
Camber Castle	TQ 922185	....p 7
Winchelsea Church	TQ 904173	....p 7

Map 197:
*CHICHESTER & THE DOWNS (extends north of
MIDHURST and east of ARUNDEL)*

Amberley Castle	TQ 027132	....p 9
Bankside, Burpham (John Cowper Powys)	TQ 039089	.....p 9
Market Cross, Chichester	SU 861048	....p 17
Chichester Cathedral...............................	SU 859048	....p 17,29
St Mary's Hospital Almshouses	SU 862050	....p 17
Site of Roman amphitheatre, Chichester	SU 867046	....p 17
11 Eastgate Square, Chichester...(Keats)	SU 866045	....p 17
Guildhall Museum, Chichester ..(Blake)	SU 860048	....p 17
Blake's Cottage, Felpham	SZ 951997	....p 17
Fishbourne Roman Palace	SU 840052	....p 17
Weald & Downland Open Air Museum	SU 875128	p 17,53,79
Tangmere Military Aviation Museum ..	SU 906061	....p 17
The Black Rabbit, Arundel	TQ 026085	....p 23
Houghton Bridge......................................	TQ 026118	....p 23,59
Bury footbridge.......................................	TQ 017130	....p 23
Greatham Bridge ....:	TQ 032163	....p 23
Medieval bridge, Trotton	SU 836224	....p 23
Medieval bridge, Stopham	TQ 030183	....p 23
Amberley Wildbrooks	TQ 030140	....p 23
Chalk Pits Museum, Amberley	TQ 031123	....p 23,53
Bignor Roman Villa	SU 987147	....p 23
Parham House..	TQ 060143	....p 23,69
Arundel Castle	TQ 018073	....p 23,57
Granary, Eastergate	SU 945051	....p 29
North Mundham Church (Sussex marble)	SU 875022	....p 29
Kirdford Church ....(Sussex marble)	TQ 018265	....p 29
Woolbeding House ....(Charlotte Smith)	SU 872222	....p 29
Bury House ....(John Galsworthy)	TQ 011132	....p 31
The Swan, Lower Fittleworth	TQ 010185	....p 33
Drunkenness plaque, Kirdford..............	TQ 018266	....p 33
Chichester Harbour Conservancy..........	SU 799014	....p 35
East Head nature reserve	SZ 766990	....p 35
Bosham Church...	SU 804039	....p 35
Pagham Harbour nature reserve............	SZ 857965	....p 35
Bognor Regis pier	SZ 935987	....p 39
Lurgashall Church................(Tennyson)	SU 938273)	....p 45
Spread Eagle Inn, Midhurst	SU 886215	....p 49
Cowdray Ruins, Midhurst	SU 891217	....p 49
Chemist's shop, Midhurst (H.G. Wells)	SU 887215	....p 49
Midhurst Grammar School(H.G. Wells)	SU 886218	....p 49
Tea shop, Midhurst ....(H.G. Wells)	SU 886216	....p 49
Uppark, South Harting......(H.G. Wells)	SU 779177	....p 49,69
Rycroft, Burpham ..(Tickner Edwardes)	TQ 040089	....p 51
Ilex Cottage, Burpham ....(Edwardes)	TQ 044090	....p 51
Burpham churchyard(Edwardes, Peake)	TQ 039090	....p 51,57
Kithurst Hill	TQ 082125	....p 55
Rackham Hill	TQ 053126	....p 55
Bignor Hill	SU 983136	....p 55
Burton Down..	SU 966132	....p 55
Littleton Down..	SU 942150	....p 55
Treyford Hill	SU 830177	....p 55

WHEN THEY WROTE WHAT THEY WROTE

This list, which is not exhaustive, gives authors' lifespans and/or the original publication dates of individual works:

George Aitchison (*Sussex* 1936); F.R. Banks (*Penguin Guides - Sussex* 1957); Arthur Beckett (*The Spirit of the Downs* 1909); Hilaire Belloc (1870-1953, *The Four Men* 1912); E.F. Benson (1867-1940); Wilfrid Scawen Blunt (1840-1922); Dirk Bogarde (*A Postillion Struck by Lightning* 1977); Peter Brandon (*The Sussex Landscape* 1974); Lillian Candlin (*Tales of Old Sussex* 1985, *Memories of Old Sussex* 1987); Harold Cannings (*Follow the Plough* 1992); Brigid Chapman (*Sussex - A Portrait in Colour* 1989, *Night of the Fires* 1994); Alec Clifton-Taylor (*Six More English Towns* 1981); William Cobbett (1763-1835); A.E. Coppard (1878-1957, *It's Me, O Lord!* 1957); Bob Copper (*A Song for Every Season* 1971, *Early to Rise* 1976, *Across Sussex With Belloc* 1994); Ben Darby (*View of Sussex* 1975, *The South Downs* 1976, *Journey Through the Weald* 1986); Frank Dean (*Strike While the Iron's Hot* 1994); Tickner Edwardes (1865-1944, *A Country Calendar* 1928, *A Downland Year* 1939); John Coker Egerton (*Sussex Folk & Sussex Ways* 1892); Jim Etherington (*Lewes Bonfire Night* 1993); John Galsworthy (1867-1933); Angelica Garnett (*Deceived With Kindness* 1984); Eve Garnett (*In and Out and Roundabout* 1948); Stella Gibbons (*Cold Comfort Farm* 1932); Eric Gill (1882-1940, *Autobiography* 1940); Graham Greene (*Brighton Rock* 1938); Marguerite Radcylffe Hall (1883-1943); John Halsham [George Forrester Scott] (1853-1937); W.H.Hudson (1841-1922, *Nature in Downland* 1900); Henry James (1843-1916); Richard Jefferies (1848-1887); Sheila Kaye-Smith (1887-1956); Rudyard Kipling (1865-1936); Peter Linklater (*Lewes Twittens* 1991); Mark Antony Lower (1813-1876); E.V. Lucas (1868-1938, *Highways & Byways in Sussex* 1935); S.P.B. Mais (1885-1975, *Sussex* 1950); Arthur Mee (*The King's England* 1937); Esther Meynell (*Sussex* 1947); A.A. Milne (1882-1956, *The House at Pooh Corner* 1928); Christopher Milne (*The Enchanted Places* 1974); William Morris (1834-1896); Ian Nairn/Nikolaus Pevsner (*The Buildings of England - Sussex* 1965); Rev W.D. Parish (1833-1904, *A Dictionary of the Sussex Dialect* 1875); Coventry Patmore (1823-1896); Mervyn Peake (1911-1968, *Titus Groan* 1946); Evelyn Pentecost (*A Shepherd's Daughter* 1987); John Cowper Powys (1872-1963); Vera G. Pragnell (*The Story of the Sanctuary* 1928); Maude Robinson (*A South Down Farm in the Sixties* 1938); Gilbert Sargent (*A Sussex Life* 1989); Desmond Seward (*Sussex* 1995); Charlotte Smith (1748-1806); William Carter Swan (*The Diary of a Farm Apprentice* 1984); Alfred, Lord Tennyson (1809-1892); Edward Thomas (1878-1917, *The South Country* 1909); Len Tuppen (*Only Yesterday* 1991); Tony Wales (*A Sussex Garland* 1979); Gilbert White (1720-1793); Walter Wilkinson (*A Sussex Peepshow* 1933); Barbara Willard (*The Forest* 1989); Barclay Wills (*Bypaths in Downland* 1927, *Downland Treasure* 1929); Viscountess Wolseley (*Sussex in the Past* 1928); Frederick W. Wood (*Round About Sussex Downs* 1925).

INDEX